KNITTING
TECHNIQUES

KINGFISHER

PRACTICAL GUIDES

KNITTING TECHNIQUES

MARGARET MAINO

Kingfisher Books

Kingfisher Books, Grisewood & Dempsey Ltd,
Elsley House, 24–30 Great Titchfield Street,
London W1P 7AD

First published in 1990 by Kingfisher Books

British Library Cataloguing in Publication Data
More, Hilary
    Dressmaking techniques.
    1. Women's clothing. Making
    I. Title
    646.404

    ISBN 0-86272-544-5

Senior Editor: Janice Lacock
Editorial Assistant: Sophie Figgis

Phototypeset by Southern Positives and
Negatives (SPAN), Lingfield, Surrey
Printed in Yugoslavia

CONTENTS

Introduction

There is arguably no substitute for being shown how to knit by a kind and patient relative or friend. Unfortunately the skills that were commonplace in our grandparents' times are no longer passed down from generation to generation. However, if you are interested, and perhaps with some guidance from a willing friend, it is certainly possible to teach yourself to knit.

This book guides beginners through the first steps in mastering the art of knitting and describes all the techniques in common use. Yet the book's usefulness is not limited to those just starting out: it is a comprehensive reference guide for all knitters. Experienced knitters will find plenty of advice and handy tips for improving their knitting skills and achieving a more professional-looking finish. The compact size of the book means that you can carry it around with you, so slip the book in with your knitting and you will always find help close at hand.

It is impossible to describe the intricacies of knitting with words alone, even a single drawing in some cases is quite inadequate. Throughout this book you will therefore find plenty of step-by-step diagrams showing techniques, and photographs illustrating the finished result.

To help you find your way about this book it is split into logical sections beginning with information and explanations of basic techniques (so that everything the beginner needs to know is at the front). Gradually more advanced skills are introduced until you reach the specialist types of knitting towards the end. The book concludes with details of making up a garment and caring for it afterwards.

One of the most difficult aspects of writing a book on knitting techniques is deciding which to include – and which to leave out. Knitting aficionados probably know that there are numerous ways to cast on, cast off or do so many things. With some technique books there are so many alternative methods to choose from that it is hard to pick the appropriate one. I have therefore selected the major techniques, plus some interesting alternatives that you might like to consider . . . certainly more than enough to guide you through most of the knitting situations that you will encounter. (How did I make this choice? Well, anything that I had not used in a 'lifetime' of knitting was counted as being too specialist for everyday use.) I hope you will enjoy experimenting with the techniques given here.

Margaret Mano

Yarns

Yarn is a generic term for any type of thread used as knitting material regardless of how it is produced. Yarns consist of either one or a series of fibres, which are obtained from all over the world, to make the rich, and often bewildering, array that is available in the shops today.

There are two main categories of fibre – natural (divided into animal and vegetable origins) and synthetics (those which are man-made). Both types possess characteristic qualities – in general, natural fibres 'breathe', giving good insulation and absorption so making them pleasant to wear and 'handle' (how a yarn feels to the touch) during knitting. Synthetics are stronger and more durable, but mainly cheaper than natural fibres, some of which are in short supply and therefore very expensive. A third category of fibre consists of clever mixes of synthetic and natural fibres combining the best qualities of each to make strong, reliable yarns that are lightweight and pleasant to handle.

The following list describes the main fibres that you will come across, where they originate and what qualities you can expect from them. They are divided into natural fibres derived from animals and vegetables, and synthetic fibres.

Natural Fibres Derived from Animals
Wool
Regardless of fashion and the economic climate, wool has always dominated the knitting industry. Sheep are bred specifically for their fleeces, particularly Merinos which have the most abundant and highest quality wool.

Qualities Easily available, elastic, long-lasting, has excellent insulation due to the natural 'crimp' in the fibres, and is absorbent so making it comfortable to wear.

Provenance Australia, Soviet Union, New Zealand, China and Argentina.

Mohair
This fluffy yarn has become a classic fashion fibre. It comes from an angora goat, although the 'angora' part of the name is confusing as it has nothing to do with angora yarn (see below), but denotes the region of Turkey from which the goats originate. Fibres are very fragile so a pure mohair yarn is rare; normally there is a percentage of wool or other fibres to strengthen it.

Qualities Long, brushed fibres are extremely thick and warm, with a luxurious appearance.

Provenance South Africa and Texas.

Angora
A rare and expensive fibre, angora comes from an albino rabbit of the same name. The hair is mostly short and slippery, making it difficult to spin without the addition of other fibres.

○ The high-quality wool from Merino sheep accounts for the majority of the world's production.

Qualities Extremely soft and warm with a silky handle and a light, fuzzy appearance. Beware if you are allergic to animal hairs – short hairs of angora shed easily.
Provenance China – in very short supply.

Cashmere
The most luxurious of fibres, cashmere is produced from the hair of a special breed of goat that survives the rigours of life in

Central Asia. Demand for this special fibre is always high, supplies are scarce and therefore the yarn is extremely expensive. As the cost of pure cashmere would be prohibitive, most cashmere yarns contain a high percentage of wool.

Qualities Very soft and warm without the hairiness of other luxury yarns.

Provenance Mainly China – in very short supply.

○ The alpaca's soft coat yields a fine luxury yarn.

Alpaca

Another fibre at the luxury end of the market, alpaca comes from an animal of the same name. The alpaca is a species of camel, closely-related to the llama, which lives at high altitudes in the Andes of South America.

Qualities A soft, high quality fibre with a slight hairiness.

Provenance South America, particularly Peru and Bolivia.

Silk

The silk worm produces a continuous filament when it constructs a cocoon. Special processing enables the filament to be unwound intact from the cocoon and spun into silk. They are a luxury, but pure silk knitting yarns can give problems since the

○ The technique of spinning silk was pioneered in China.

ideal, tightly twisted yarn is heavy (therefore expensive) which causes the garment to drop. Look out for mixtures of yarn with both synthetic and natural fibres that give interesting effects without the drawbacks.

Qualities A light fibre, yet strong enough to be spun very finely. Non-conductive to heat, therefore suitable for all seasons. Less elastic than wool.

Provenance Once a monopoly of China, but now produced world-wide.

Natural Fibres Derived from Vegetables
Cotton
This is a natural plant fibre that can be harvested and spun into a yarn with exceptional strength. Knitting yarns are often mercerized – a chemical process that improves the quality by adding lustre and preventing further shrinkage.

Cotton has become very popular in recent years in the hand-knitting market and a large variety of weights, textures and mixtures with other fibres is available. Remember that cotton has very little elasticity: you must work at an even tension or irregularities will be obvious, especially in a colour pattern. Ribbed welts may also need knitting elastic to help them keep their shape.

Qualities Strong, versatile, non-allergenic and absorbent; easy to wash and wear.
Provenance Soviet Union, U.S.A., China and India.

○ Cotton picking is still carried out by hand in some parts of the world.

Linen
The flax plant is grown specifically for producing linen fibres. These are very strong, even more so than cotton fibres, but have no elasticity. Most yarns containing linen have been blended with other, more elastic fibres such as wool.
Qualities Extremely strong, durable and absorbent.
Provenance Can be grown in any region with the right climatic conditions – a rich soil and damp weather. Ireland and Belgium are noted for linen.

Chunky

Aran

Double knitting

4-ply

3-ply

2-ply

Synthetic Fibres

Man-made fibres are known as synthetics. Originally synthetic yarns were synonymous with 'cheap and nasty'. They were hard and harsh to wear with a 'lifeless' quality about them. However, recent years have seen much research and development in this field by the major chemical companies, many of whom call their products by specific names rather than the general terms of 'acrylic' or 'polyamide'.

Tweed

Marled

Slub

Mohair

Crepe

Bouclé

Today clever combinations of synthetic and natural fibres produce yarns of a very high standard – strong, lightweight and versatile. They are hard-wearing, easy to wash and competitively priced against the more expensive natural fibres.

Spinning

This is the process of manufacturing yarn for hand knitting. Modern advances in spinning techniques have encouraged the growth of many fancy yarn effects. The predominant trend in knitted garments is for quite simple styles where the main interest is provided by fancy textured, multi-coloured yarns. Apart from the fibres involved, other important factors at the spinning stage include the ply (thickness), texture and colour.

Ply

Yarn is formed by twisting together a number of strands of fibre. A 'ply' is the term for one of these strands and it is used as a measure of the thickness of the yarn. The following plies – from thin to thick – are readily available: 3 ply, 4 ply, double knitting, Aran (triple knitting), chunky (double double knitting) and extra chunky (see p.13). Unfortunately the ply can only be a general guide to the thickness when substituting yarns as the measurement of a single ply is not standard.

Texture

During the spinning process textures can be created by varying the speed and tension at which different fibres are fused together. **Bouclé** is the common term for three types of highly-textured yarn – true bouclé, gimp and loop. In all of these types one of the plies is introduced at a faster rate than the others so that it buckles up. **Mohair** is originally a loop yarn. Brushing the yarn breaks the loops to give it a fluffy appearance. **Slub** yarns have at least one ply that varies in thickness so that when it is added to another of regular thickness an uneven effect results. **Tweed** effects are formed by adding coloured 'blips' (called knops) to the longer fibres. **Crepe** yarns are more tightly twisted during spinning to produce, when knitted, a smooth fabric with a characteristic pebbled surface.

Colour

Special effects in the dyeing process make yarns even more interesting. **Solid colour** is a consistent single colour through-out. The choice of colour can effect the weight of the yarn – dark colours obviously use a lot of dye, which makes the yarn heavier and also thinner. **Heather mixtures** are produced when strands are separately dyed and subtle colours are blended before spinning. **Twists** are plies of very different colours used together. **Ombré** is a shaded effect where patches of one colour appear at intervals.

Buying and Using Yarn

When you consider the hours spent knitting a garment, it is worthwhile buying the best yarn you can afford so it will give you lasting pleasure and service. If economy is the keynote of your knitting, then there are plenty of bargains to be found.

Yarn bought in a shop is enclosed in a wrapper known as a 'ball band'. Apart from obvious details such as the names of the yarn and the manufacturer and the weight, you should also find plenty of other useful information on the ball band. This should include: *fibre content* – a list and percentage of fibres (check if you are allergic to any); *a recommended tension and needle size* – suggested as a number of stitches and rows to a given measurement and worked in stocking stitch (this is a guide only; when working a pattern you must always match the tension stated in the pattern); *washing and cleaning instructions* – file a ball band for future reference (if you know that you are unlikely to hand wash your knitteds, choose a yarn that is machine-washable or one that can be dry cleaned).

The colour of the yarn is stated as a 'shade number' on the ball band, as well as the 'dye lot'. Yarn is dyed in batches; as shades can vary slightly between dye lots (this can be very obvious in a finished garment), it is important that you buy the complete amount you require from the same batch. Many yarn shops will allow you to reserve a few balls to be collected only if you need them, or to return unused balls.

Most hand knitting yarns are now available in balls or doughnuts (a softer, squashed shape often used for brushed or speciality yarns). The natural inclination is to start knitting with the end of yarn that is on the outside. However, using the end of yarn from the inside of the ball is less troublesome as it prevents twists. Remove the ball band, then find the inner end by poking down through the centre of the ball. You may have to remove a small amount of yarn from the centre before finding the end, but once you have done that you should be able to slip the ball band back on again.

78% MOHAIR
13% WOOL
9% NYLON
SHADE 596
LOT 1269

50% WOOL
50% ACRYLIC
ACRYLIQUE
POLYACRYL

SUITABLE FOR ANY

Needle Conversion Chart

Metric	(Old) English	American
2 mm	14	0
2¼ mm	13	1
2¾ mm	12	2
3 mm	11	
3¼ mm	10	3
3¾ mm	9	5
4 mm	8	6
4½ mm	7	7
5 mm	6	8
5½ mm	5	9
6 mm	4	10
6½ mm	3	10½
7 mm	2	
7½ mm	1	
8 mm	0	11
9 mm	00	13
10 mm	000	15

Equipment

Knitting requires few basic tools, all of which are relatively inexpensive to buy. Everybody knows that knitting is worked on needles, but you may be surprised at the range of complimentary accessories – some essential and others merely useful – that are available. Check that your work box contains the essential ingredients before you begin knitting, then as your skills improve you might be interested in adding the optional extras.

Needles

Modern needles are made from coated aluminium, plastic or wood, all of which are light and easy to work with. The material makes no difference to your work, so choosing is a matter of personal preference. All needles are practically maintenance-free; an occasional wash will remove stickiness due to handling.

The size of a needle is a metric measurement taken around the body of the shaft: there are 17 stages from 10mm down to 2mm. Metric measurements are now common in Britain and throughout the Continent. However confusion can arise with the previous English system of numbering needles (many of which are still in existence) and the American system, which is totally different. The chart shown here is a guide to converting needle sizes. Needles are available in different forms for specific tasks.

Pairs of needles For flat knitting in rows you need a pair of needles with a blunt point at one end and a knob at the other end to stop the stitches falling off. Needles are available in three lengths – 25, 30 and 35cm (approximately 10, 12 and 14in). The ideal length is a matter of personal choice, depending on your style of working. If your work involves a large number of stitches, then you will cope better with a long pair of needles; otherwise, it is generally more relaxing to work with shorter ones.

Circular needles These can be used for circular knitting (a method of knitting in the round to make a circular fabric without seams) or for flat knitting worked in rows where a large number of stitches is involved. Two stiff needle ends are linked by a piece of flexible nylon cord. Again, different lengths (of cord) are available according to the number of stitches that you are dealing with. If you have only a few stitches in a piece of circular knitting, a long circular needle is no good as it would mean too great a stretch to join the stitches into a circle. Patterns for circular knitting usually specify the length of needle as well as the size.

Double-pointed needles Usually available in sets of four, these needles are used for circular knitting, particularly for small items such as gloves, socks and hats, which require only a small number of stitches. The total number of stitches is divided between three of the needles and the fourth is used for working.

Sewing needles

Tape measure

Crochet hooks

Scissors

Graph paper

Pins

Bobbins

Double-pointed
needles

Cable needles

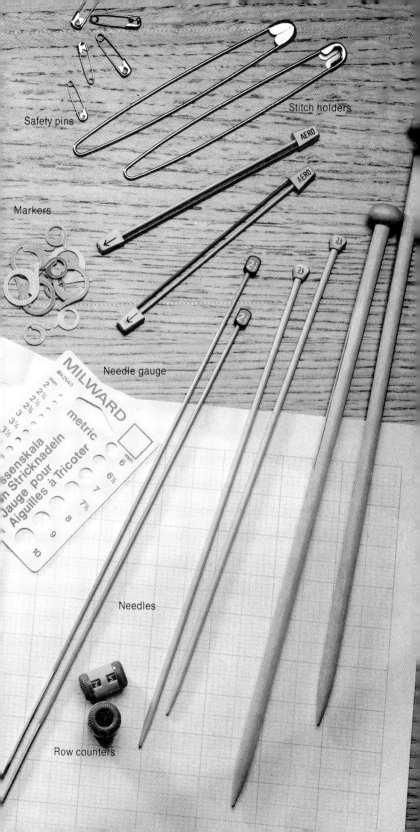

Safety pins

Stitch holders

Markers

Needle gauge

MILWARD
#42640
metric

Needles

Row counters

Essential Items
Tape measure
Buy a good quality dressmaker's tape. If the measurements are in both metric and imperial, use one system throughout. A rigid ruler is also extremely useful when measuring, especially for small areas like tension swatches.

Stitch holders
It is often necessary at some stage in a garment to keep stitches 'on hold' until you need to work on them again. To prevent these stitches unravelling slip them on to a holder. Holders are available in various forms, but they all have a fastening at one end; choose ones that feel most secure.

Scissors
At the end of a piece of work many patterns say 'break off yarn' which implies that you can easily do this by hand. In fact, as many yarns contain strong fibres, you should always cut the yarn with a pair of scissors. These can be quite small, but must always be sharp.

Pins
If pins are too small, they will be obscured by the knitted fabric. Long (5cm/2in) dressmaker's pins or glass-headed pins are the best choice for measuring out tension, blocking out a section of work for pressing, and pinning pieces together when sewing up.

Sewing needles
Also known as 'yarn' or 'tapestry' needles, they must be blunt-ended (or they will split the yarn) with a large 'eye' in relation to the type of yarn being used; very thick yarn can be damaged by forcing it through a needle that is too small.

Work bag
To protect your work in progress and save time searching for all the related items, you need something to store them in. It is easy to buy a purpose-made bag, although any large receptacle will do as long as it is easy to carry. Beware of using thin plastic carriers; knitting needles soon poke through and can be extremely dangerous, especially if the bag is then left where somebody could fall on it.

Useful Items
Cable needles
These needles are used for holding stitches being transferred from one position to another during the working of the cables. There are two types – short, straight double-pointed needles or short needles with a curve or angle in the centre to stop the stitches falling off. Choose a size that corresponds to the

thickness of your yarn – or one that is slightly finer as too thick needles can stretch the stitches.

Row counter
A row counter is a handy cylindrical attachment that slips on to the end of a needle. You wind on the figures to keep track of the number of rows you have knitted.

Needle gauge
A plastic needle gauge is useful for checking needle sizes, particularly circular and double-pointed needles where there is no indication of size. Simply insert the body of the needle into a hole – the correct one is the smallest that it fits into.

Bobbins
If you frequently work colour patterns, stop the yarns tangling by investing in plastic bobbins for holding small amounts of yarn wound off from the main ball. Bobbins made from card are also efficient (see p.150).

Crochet hooks
It is worthwhile owning a few hooks in small, medium and large sizes. Crochet finishing touches to a knitted design are sometimes called for, and a hook is also a useful tool for picking up dropped stitches (see p.171).

Teasel brush
Mohair and brushed yarns are very popular. Their pile flattens with handling during knitting, but you can restore it by brushing with this small wire brush.

Markers
Small, circular plastic loops that can be clipped on to a stitch so that it can be identified at a later stage are also handy.

Safety pins
Varying in size from small (ideal for fine yarns and baby garments) to medium and large, safety pins make a multi-purpose addition to your work bag. Use them principally as stitch holders where only a small number of stitches are being held, or to secure a dropped stitch until you are able to deal with it.

Needle stops
The sharp points of needle tips are potentially dangerous, especially if somebody falls on them. To protect the tips when the needles are not in use and to prevent overcrowded stitches falling off the needle, you can buy needle tip protectors. Alternatively, use corks from a bottle or elastic bands wound round and round the point.

Working from a Pattern

Most knitting patterns are produced by yarn manufacturers (spinners) or appear as magazine editorials. Although the style in which patterns are presented may vary slightly according to the publisher, there are basic similarities. All contain general information (sizes, materials, tension, abbreviations), written or charted instructions and details of how to assemble the garment. Everything is presented in a logical order to help the knitter, but it is important that you read the pattern through before you begin knitting so that you have a general understanding of the work. Some details or instructions may not be entirely clear on first reading; in this case it probably involves a technique which will become obvious when the work is in front of you.

(illustrated in Diploma Chunky, Shade 9721 in size 86 cm on an 86 cm model)

3202
Scarf: Cobwebs, Islington Park St.
Trousers: Hudson and Hudson at Hyper Hyper

V NECK SWEATER

To fit bust						
81	86	91	**97**	102	**107**	cm
32	**34**	36	38	40	42	in (approx)

Actual size						
99	**104**	110	**116**	120	**126**	cm
39	**41**	43½	**45½**	47	**49½**	in (approx)

Patons Diploma Chunky						
15	**16**	17	**18**	19	50 gram balls

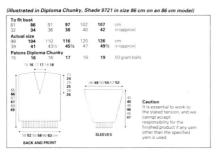

BACK AND FRONT

SLEEVES

Caution
It is essential to work to the stated tension, and we cannot accept responsibility for the finished product if any yarn other than the specified yarn is used.

Quantities of yarn are approximate as they are based on average requirements.
Although every effort is made to ensure that the colours on this leaflet are true representations of their respective yarns, they may not always exactly match due to technical restrictions of printing processes.

Pair each Nos 4½ mm and 6 mm needles. Cable pin

Tension
On No 6 mm needles, 15 sts and 20 rows to 10 cm (stocking st). Panel patt (12 sts) measures 6 cm when slightly stretched.

Abbreviations
K = knit; P = purl; st = stitch; tog = together; alt = alternate; sL1K = slip 1 knitways; psso = pass slipped stitch over; inc = increase by working into front and back of stitch; stocking st = stocking stitch (1 row knit, 1 row purl); beg = beginning; dec = decrease by working 2 tog; stocking st = stocking stitch (1 row knit, 1 row purl); patt = pattern; rep = repeat; cm = centimetres; in = inches; mm = millimetres; tbl = through back of loops; C8B = cable 8 back worked thus: slip next 4 sts onto cable pin and leave at back of work, K4, then K4 from cable pin. C4B = cable 4 back worked thus: slip next 2 sts onto cable pin and leave at back of work, K2, then K2 from cable pin; C4F = cable 4 front worked thus: slip next 2 sts onto cable pin and leave at front of work, K2, then K2 from cable pin; M1 = make a stitch by picking up horizontal loop lying before next stitch and working into back of it.
N.B. DO NOT "MAKE 1" by knitting into the front and back of a stitch.

Instructions are given for the first size, with larger sizes given in square brackets []. Where only one figure is given this applies to all sizes.

PANEL PATT (12 sts)

1st row—(Right side) P2, K8, P2.
2nd row—K2, P8, K2
3rd row—P2, C8B, P2
4th row—as above
5th to 18th rows—Rep 1st and 2nd rows 7 times more.
19th row—As 3rd.
20th row—As 2nd.
21st and 22nd rows—As 1st and 2nd
These 22 rows form panel patt.

BACK

With No 4½ mm needles cast on 61[65, 69, 73, 77, 81] sts and work in rib as follows:
1st row—(Right side). K1, * P1, K1, rep from * to end.
2nd row—P1, * K1, P1, rep from * to end.
Rep these 2 rows for 8 cm, ending with a 1st row *****
Next row—Rib 7[3, 5, 2, 3, 5], * M1, rib 4[5, 5, 5, 6, 6], rep from * to last 6[2, 4, 1, 2, 4] sts, M1, rib to end .(74[78, 82, 88, 90, 94] sts).
Change to No 6 mm needles and work in stocking st until Back measures 65[66, 67, 67, 68, 69] cm, ending with a P row
Shape shoulders by casting off 9[9, 9, 10, 10, 11] sts at beg of next 4 rows and 8[9, 10, 11, 11, 11] sts at beg of following 2 rows.
Leave remaining 22[24, 26, 26, 28, 28] sts on a holder.

FRONT

Work as given for Back to ******
Next row—Rib 5[7, 9, 4, 6, 8], * M1, rib 4[4, 4, 5, 5, 5], * rep from * to 5 times more, (M1, rib 1) 4 times, rep from * to * 6 times, M1, rib to end (78[82, 86, 90, 94, 98] sts).
Change to No 6 mm needles and work in patt as follows:
1st row—(Right side). K33[35, 37, 39, 41, 43] panel patt as 1st row across next 12 sts, K33[35, 37, 39, 41, 43].
2nd row—P33[35, 37, 39, 41, 43], panel patt as 2nd row across next 12 sts, P33[35, 37, 39, 41, 43].
Continue thus working appropriate rows of panel patt until Front measures approximately 41 cm, ending with a 22nd row of panel patt.
Divide for neck as follows:
Next row—K33[35, 37, 39, 41, 43], P2, K4, pick up loop lying between st just worked and next st on left hand needle, P into back, then P into front of it, K4, P2, K to end.
Next row—P33[35, 37, 39, 41, 43], K2, P4, K1, turn and leave remaining sts on a spare needle
Work in patt as follows:
1st row—P1, C4F, P2, sL1K, K1, psso, K to end.
2nd row—P32[34, 36, 38, 40, 42], K2, P4, K1.
3rd row—P1, K4, P2, K to end.
4th row—As 2nd row.
5th row—P1, K4, P2, sL1K, K1, psso, K to end.
6th row—P31[33, 35, 37, 39, 41] K2, P4, K1

Continue to cable on next and every following 6th row, **at the same time**, dec 1 st within the border on every 4th row from previous dec until 30[31, 32, **35**, 35, **37**] sts remain. Work straight until Front measures same as Back to shoulder, ending with wrong side facing for next row.
Shape shoulder by casting off 9[9, 9, 10, 10, **11**] sts at beg of next and following alt row. Work 1 row. **Next row**—P1, [P2tog and cast off] 3 times, cast off remaining sts.

Return to sts on spare needle
With **wrong** side of work facing, rejoin yarn to remaining sts, then work as follows: K1, P4, K2, P to end
1st row—K31[33, 35, **37**, 39, **41**], K2tog, P2, C4B, P1 **2nd row**—K1, P4, K2, P to end
3rd row—K32[34, 36, 38, 40, 42], P2, K4, P1
4th row—As 2nd.
5th row—K32[34, 36, 38, 40], K2tog, P2, k4, P1. **6th row**—As 2nd.
Continuing to cable on next and every following 6th row, **at the same time**, dec 1 st within the border on every 4th row from previous dec until 30[31, 32, **35**, 35, **37**] sts remain. Work straight until Front measures same as Back to shoulder, ending with right side facing for next row
Shape shoulder by casting off 9[9, 9, 10, 10, **11**] sts at beg of next and following alt row. Work 1 row. **Next row**—K1, [K2tog and cast off] 3 times, cast off remaining sts.

SLEEVES

With No 4½ mm needles cast on 31[31, 33, 35, 35, **37**] sts and work 7 cm in rib as on Back, ending with a 1st row
1st row—Rib 8[8, 2, 5, 5, 3], * M1, rib 1[1, 2, 2, 2], rep from * to last 8[8, 1, 4, 4, 4] sts, M1, rib to end. (47[47, 49, 49, 49, **53**] sts)
Change to 6 mm needles and work in stocking st, shaping sides by inc 1 st at each end of 9th[**3rd**, 3rd, 3rd, 11th, **5th**] and every following 6th[**6th**, 6th, 6th, 4th, **6th**] row until there are 67[71, 73, 73, 77, 77] sts.
Work straight until sleeve seam measures 45[45, 46, 46, 46, **47**] cm, ending with a P row. Cast off loosely

MAKE UP AND NECK BORDER

With wrong side of work facing, block each piece by pinning out round edges, and omitting ribbing and cables, press lightly following instructions on ball band.
Join right shoulder seam.
Neck Border—With right side facing, and No 4½ mm needles, **knit up** 50[52, 54, 54, 58, **58**] sts down left side of neck, pick up loop at centre V and knit into back of it (mark this st with a coloured thread), **knit up** 50[52, 54, 54, 58, **58**] sts up right side of neck, then K22[24, 26, 26, 28, 28] sts from Back. (123[**129**, 135, 135, 145, **145**] sts).
1st row—* P1, K1, rep from * to within 2 sts of marked st, P2tog, P1, P2togtbl, ** P1, rep from * to end.
2nd row—K1, * P1, K1, rep from * to within 2 sts of marked st, P2tog, K1, P2togtbl, K1, ** * P1, K1, rep from * to end.
Rep these 2 rows twice more, then 1st row again. Cast off evenly in rib, dec as before.
Join left shoulder seam and Neck Border
Place centre of cast off edges of sleeves to shoulder seams and sew sleeves in position to front and back. Join side and sleeve seams.

We shall be happy to deal with your queries if you write to Sarah Bell, Patons & Baldwins Limited, Alloa, Scotland, enclosing a ball band of the yarn specified and a stamped addressed envelope.

PUBLISHED BY PATONS & BALDWINS LIMITED

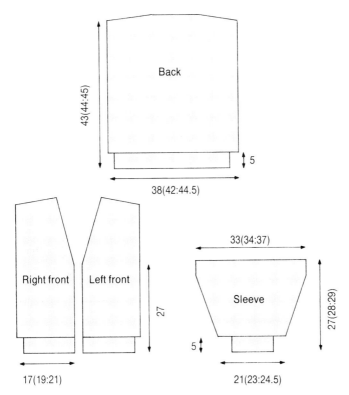

Tempting as it may be, do not choose a design that is too difficult for your capabilities. It is quite likely that you will become frustrated and abandon the project.

Sizes

Sizing usually includes chest or bust and other major measurements such as length and sleeve seam. A pattern may be written in a variety of sizes; instructions for the first size are given outside a set of brackets (parentheses) with the larger sizes following on in order within the brackets.

When choosing the size to make, look for the *actual* measurement of the finished garment. The amount of ease ('room') in a garment varies according to the style, although it is generally 5–10cm (2–4in). You may prefer to make a smaller size than normal if the finished result for your size is too baggy for your taste. Once you have decided on a size, keep track of it by marking relevant figures throughout the pattern.

Measurement diagrams are a recent inclusion on many patterns. These are scale drawings of the pattern pieces with more detailed measurements that allow you to see at a glance their shape and size. Diagrams are a useful guide when you are measuring your knitting during the blocking and pressing process (see pp.173–4).

Patterns to beware of

○ Patterns that say to fit size 86cm bust, but do not indicate the *actual* width. Your idea of the amount of ease you like in a garment may not coincide with that of the designers.

○ Patterns that are only available in one size – which is quite likely to be totally unflattering to your size.

○ 'Speedy to knit' designs that are billed as being made in a few hours. Generally these knits are based on giant needles and loose stitches: the resulting fabric will stretch and stretch.

Choosing and substituting yarns

A design is created by a spinner for the purpose of selling a particular brand of yarn. Every knitter will be aware of the frustration of being unable to obtain the yarn stated in a pattern, or perhaps preferring an alternative – a cotton rather than a wool or synthetic.

Although there are frequently severe warnings against substitution, it may be possible if you are aware of the pitfalls. Most commercial yarns have a recommended tension printed on the ball band; for an alternative choice, if this tension is the same as that stated in the pattern then there should be no problems providing that you make the usual tension swatch with the substitute yarn as a final check.

Choosing yarn for beginners

○ If the type of yarn called for in the pattern is new to you, initially buy a single ball and practise to see if you like knitting with it.

○ You will obviously see fast results from working with thick yarns. However, if you choose one that is too thick you will find it difficult to handle on the needles.

○ A yarn with a slight 'hairiness' or a 'fuzzy' effect can help to mask the appearance of uneven stitches.

○ To begin with avoid yarns that have very little elasticity, such as cotton.

With the availability of such a large range of yarns, you must bear in mind the suitability of the substituted yarn for the style of garment. It is obvious that a textured, tweed yarn is not a good choice for a summer top, but remember that textured and brushed yarns obscure a lot of detail so they are not sensible for Arans and other stitch patterns. Changing yarns could mean that you come unstuck with the *amount* required even though both yarns may be packaged in the same weight balls. Due to the composition of the fibres each type of yarn has a different metreage – the actual length of yarn in each ball. Use the original amounts as a guide, but be aware that you may need more of a brushed or textured yarn if the yarn used in the original design is fairly smooth.

Tension

To guarantee that your knitting will be the correct size you must make a tension swatch as shown on pp.35–6. If you are unable to achieve the correct row and stitch tension together, then concentrate on getting the stitch tension right (if the row tension is a problem, avoid patterns with complicated shaping or ones that are measured in rows rather than by centimetres).

Tension variations also affect the fabric – too tight and it will be stiff and matted; too loose and it will make a garment that is likely to drop and grow out of shape.

Abbreviations

Explaining all the details in pattern writing can take up a great deal of space so a knitting shorthand of abbreviations has evolved. There are differences in style according to individual designers, writers or spinners: it is always best to read through the list that is printed before the start of every pattern. The following abbreviations are standard in most knitting patterns and are used throughout this book. Where other, more complicated techniques are explained their abbreviated form will be given at the same time.

alt – alternate(ly); beg – begin(ning); cm – centimetre(s); cont – continue(ing); dec – decrease(ing); foll – following; g st – garter stitch (every row K); inc – increase(ing); K – knit; K-wise – knitwise; P – purl; patt – pattern; psso – pass slipped stitch over; P-wise – purlwise; rem – remain(ing); rep – repeat; RS – right side; sl – slip; st(s) – stitch(es); st st – stocking stitch (1 row K, 1 row P); tbl – through back of loop(s); tog – together, WS – wrong side.

Written instructions

This section involves the main part of the pattern and describes how to knit the garment section by section, then how to assemble it. The garment sections are given under their headings (Back, Front, etc.). It is important to follow the order of knitting specified in the pattern; some pieces may have to be joined before you can continue with another stage, or instructions given out fully in one section may only be referred to briefly in another.

An asterisk (*) is a familiar symbol in a knitting pattern: it is used to avoid repetition. In a pattern row where a series of actions occurs more than once within a row, an asterisk denotes that you must repeat the sequence of stitches from that point as instructed. Brackets ( ) can also have the same effect if the stitches to be repeated are enclosed within them. A complete section of instructions may be marked out with asterisks at the beginning and end: it saves a lot of space later to refer back to this part as 'repeat from * to *'.

Accurate measurements are essential to a good piece of work, not only when checking tension, but also during the knitting process. Confusion may arise, especially where there is shaping involved, about the correct method of measuring knitting. Study the guide here and see how your own methods measure up.

Tip

○ When you are working on a 'right-side' row, the side facing you is the right side of the garment.

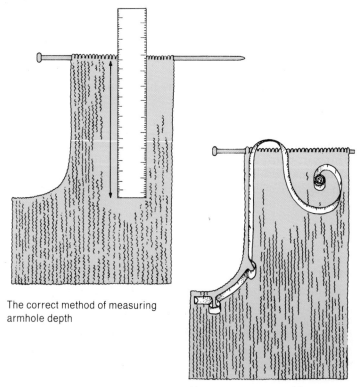

The correct method of measuring armhole depth

Never measure around the curve

Measuring knitting
In your eagerness to reach a certain point or complete a garment it is all too easy to stretch the work resulting in mismatched pieces when sewing up. Large sections of knitting, such as the main body, should be laid flat and gently smoothed out. If there are a lot of stitches bunched up on the needle, work to the middle of a row before laying it down for measuring. Unless otherwise stated the measurement should always be taken in a straight line – a long, rigid ruler is better for this job than a tape measure. When measuring an armhole, take the reading along a straight line of stitches, never around the curve. Ensure that two sleeves are exactly the same length and that the shapings correspond by knitting them simultaneously on long needles using a separate ball of yarn for each sleeve. Alternatively, use a row counter (see p.23) and make a note of how many rows you have knitted at each shaping point. Then follow this exactly for the second sleeve.

Charts
Charts often have an advantage over written instructions in that they are space saving and you can see at a glance what to do. Basically graph paper represents the knitted fabric with stitches counted across horizontally and rows vertically.

There are different types of chart – repeat patterns (see Fair Isle, pp.140–1), single motifs and colour charts (see Intarsia, p.145) and garment charts (see picture knits, p.148). Full details of working from charts are given in the chapters where they occur.

Making up a garment
Pay attention to this section; it is easy to spoil a beautifully knitted garment with careless making up. Many details about treating the yarn can be found on the ball band, and pattern instructions will tell you the order in which pieces should be sewn together. The techniques for making up garments are described and illustrated on pp.173–7.

Tips

○ Don't worry if a detail or instruction is not clear on first reading. Some techniques are only obvious when you have the actual work in front of you.

○ Charts reproduced on a small scale may be difficult to 'read'. Enlarge them on a photocopier or draw them out onto larger scale paper.

Adjusting Patterns

You may discover a pattern that you like on a knitting leaflet or in a magazine is not available in your size. Garments conform to standard sizing. If you have a specific problem such as a long body or short arms then you might be able to consider making adjustments. Alterations are fairly easy to basic designs, but they may not be viable with more complicated shapes: it is often more practical to start from scratch and re-design the garment.

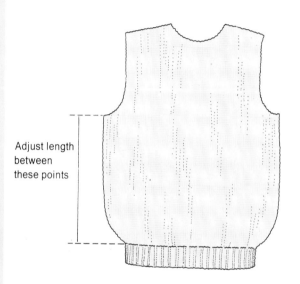

Adjust length
between
these points

Altering Basic, Plain Designs

Length is one of the simplest adjustments to make – provision for doing this may be denoted in the instructions. If the garment is drop-shouldered (i.e. has no armhole shaping) simply work the required amount more or less before commencing the shoulder shaping.

Where armhole shaping is included on the back and front, add or subtract the necessary centimetres from the straight section between the top of the welt and the start of the armholes.

Sleeves are more difficult to alter because they are generally shaped at the side edges. Use a piece of graph paper to chart out the original sleeve. Take the number of stitches after the increase row at the top of the cuff and halve it. This will allow you to draw a half section of the sleeve to save time and space, but remember to double up the number of stitches when making calculations.

Using a pencil, draw the line that represents the new sleeve top (based on your row tension) and add or subtract stitches for more or less width as necessary. Work backwards and respace all the shapings, always evenly, until they are exactly in line with the original graph.

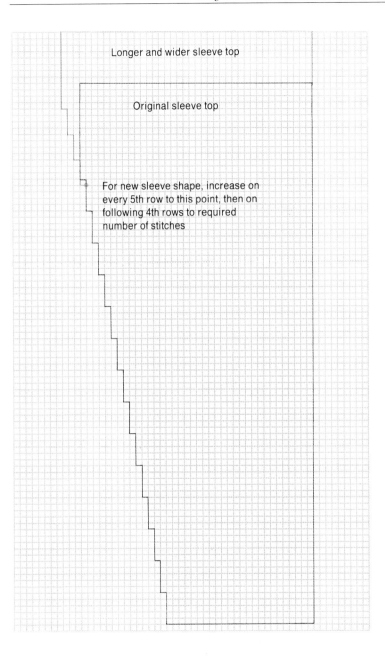

Longer and wider sleeve top

Original sleeve top

For new sleeve shape, increase on
every 5th row to this point, then on
following 4th rows to required
number of stitches

Width may be added to, or subtracted from, a section of
knitting according to the stitch tension. For example, if there are
24 stitches to 10cm, for each centimetre of difference you must
add or subtract $2\frac{1}{2}$ stitches. Usually the back and front sections

grade by 2.5cm each between sizes. To produce a larger or smaller size you would need to add or subtract 6 stitches ($2\frac{1}{2}$ stitches × 2.5 and then rounded down to nearest whole number) from those cast on. Remember to make provision for the extra or reduced stitches in the armhole, neck and shoulder shapings. As a general rule, either lose or gain one third of the difference in stitches (i.e. 2 stitches here – 1 at each armhole) in the armhole shaping, one third in the neck shaping (i.e. 2 stitches more or less cast off at the centre front or back neck) and the final third in the shoulder shaping (again 1 at either side). (The principle is the same if you are working to imperial measurements.)

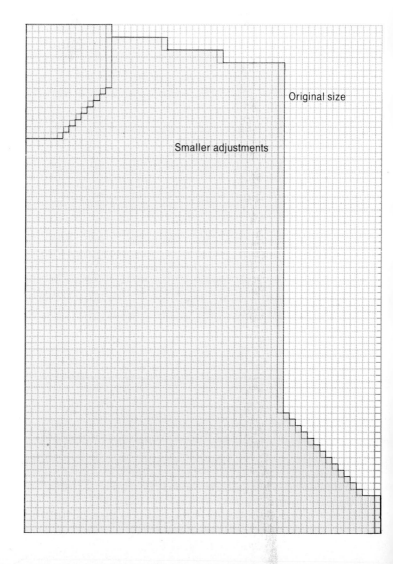

Original size

Smaller adjustments

Altering Patterned Designs

More intricate designs are not so easy to adapt. These include stitch, lace and colour patterns which involve a repeat of stitches to form the design. Often the only adjustment that can be made will involve adding or subtracting a complete repeat; the size of the garment can alter dramatically depending on the number of stitches in the repeat.

Check how the pattern will be affected by any shapings such as the armholes or neck. The best way of doing this, especially with a colour pattern, is to chart the pattern on to graph paper.

Adapting Designs

As well as making alterations to the shape of the garment, it is perfectly feasible to adapt an existing plain design by adding colour and texture patterns as well as motifs. Although few knitters would want to tackle designing a garment from scratch, there can be few who could resist taking a pattern and using it as a base for an 'original' knit incorporating their own ideas.

Colours Horizontal stripes are the simplest way of adding colour to a garment (see pp.128–9 for techniques). Stripes can be wide, narrow, regular, totally random, in two or more colours – the possibilities are endless. More advanced knitters can use intarsia techniques to create larger, more geometric designs such as checks. As long as you work in the original stitch there should be no problem with the tension.

Texture You can create surface interest with the simplest of patterned stitches, either replacing the stocking stitch entirely or worked in striped panels in conjunction with it. Either way check that the tension is compatible with the original or you may end up unwittingly altering the measurement. When working stripes of stocking stitch and texture, the textured sections may require a needle change to keep the tension even.

Motifs A simple stocking stitch sweater is an ideal background for large or small motifs placed at random or as a repeating pattern. For the best results first plot the garment shape on graph paper. Then you can mark in the motifs in their exact position, making sure that they do not encroach on any shaping.

Tips

○ Avoid alterations to a shaped sleeve top which requires a proportional combination of depth and width techniques.

○ Keep any stitches that you add (increase) in the correct pattern.

Tension

Tension (or gauge) is one of the most important aspects of knitting, yet it is so often overlooked. The stitch size of a fabric is measured by the number of stitches and rows to a given square. Before starting any work you must make sure that the fabric you produce is neither too tight or too loose. Other influences on tension include the relationship of yarn to needle sizes (see chart) and the way that you control the yarn. Knitting should be an enjoyable pastime, not a chore; relax and allow the yarn to run easily over your fingers. With practise you will notice that thicker yarns require slacker control of the tension while thinner ones need a tighter control.

Remember that the tension of your work is personal to you – any variation in control within a piece of work gives it an irregular appearance. As two people rarely work at exactly the same tension, it is unwise to let another person complete a piece of knitting you have started.

Why is tension important?

Correct tension is especially critical when you are making a garment. If you have fallen in love with a beautiful sweater, then naturally you want to reproduce it exactly. If your tension does not match that in the pattern then the sweater that you have spent so long making could end up far too big or too tiny.

The tension stated in a pattern is that achieved by the designer of the garment using the chosen yarn, needles and stitch pattern: it forms the basis of all the calculations required to give a garment its shape and size. Remember that you must be absolutely accurate in measuring your tension. It is easy to think that just one stitch out over 10cm (4in) is close enough, but that error is compounded across the width of the garment which may be 50cm (20in) (five times the tension square). Depending on the thickness of the yarn, all the extra/too few stitches can lead to a big reduction or increase in width.

There is only a small range of needle sizes appropriate to each type of yarn. The sizes shown in the chart (right) produce a knitting fabric with the correct 'handle' – soft and springy to the touch, with neat, even stitches.

Tips

○ Achieving the correct stitch tension is vital; remember that the needles stated in the pattern are only the *recommended* size and you must experiment until you find the size that works for you.

○ Most patterns are worked to a measurement rather than a number of rows. Therefore, only experiment with different needle sizes if both the stitch and row tension are inaccurate.

Type of yarn	Needle size (mm)	Typical tension (stitches/rows)
4 ply	3 $3\frac{1}{4}$ $3\frac{3}{4}$	28/36
Double knitting	$3\frac{3}{4}$ 4 $4\frac{1}{2}$	22/30
Aran	4 $4\frac{1}{2}$ 5	19/25
Chunky	5 $5\frac{1}{2}$ 6 $6\frac{1}{2}$	15/20

Making and Measuring a Tension Swatch

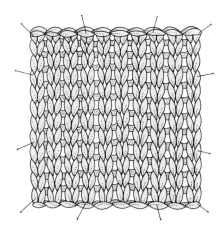

1 Make a sample swatch using the yarn and needles stated in the pattern. Tension is usually quoted over a 10cm (4in) square, but make a larger swatch (say, 12–15cm/5–6in square) as edge stitches and rows become distorted and hinder the measuring. Work in the appropriate stitch or pattern until the sample is the required length, then cast off loosely. Place the sample on a padded surface and gently smooth it into shape without stretching it. Pin the corners and sides as shown, unrolling the edges if necessary and inserting the pins at right angles to the fabric.

continued

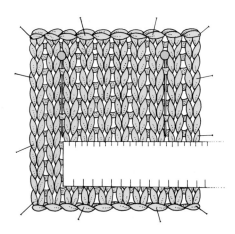

2 To assess *stitch tension,* measure horizontally across the centre of the swatch. Using pins as markers at each end, count out the number of stitches in the recommended tension. Take a rigid ruler and check the measurement between the pins – if your tension is correct, it should be 10cm (4in). Fewer stitches than stated means that your work is too loose, and more stitches that it is too tight. Be absolutely accurate with the measuring. Only one stitch out over 10cm (4in) adds up over the full width of a garment and can increase or reduce the size dramatically. If the number of stitches to 10cm (4in) is not spot on, then make another swatch using another needle size – one or two sizes smaller for work that is too loose, or larger if it is too tight.

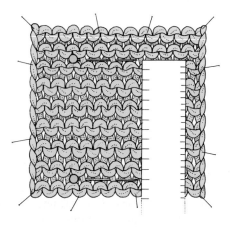

3 If the tension swatch is knitted in stocking stitch, it may be easiest to calculate the *row tension* from the reverse side of the fabric where each horizontal ridge represents one row. Follow the same procedure as given for checking stitch tension – counting out the number of rows vertically down the centre of the fabric and marking them with pins. Check the distance between the pins. If your stitch tension is correct, but the row tension is slightly out there is no need to change needle sizes.

Knitting – From the Beginning

Ancient history

Legend and facts about the origin of knitting are hard to separate, but crafts similar to knitting can be pin-pointed to the Middle East from very early times – around 1500 to 1000 BC. The earliest knitted fabric, dating from the second or third century AD, was found in Syria. However, similar fabrics from around the same time, discovered in Peru, show that the craft was probably more widespread than first thought: its tracks have been well covered with time and the lack of documentation.

Exactly how these early fabrics were produced is unclear; they could have been made on small frames, but the resulting fabric has the same structure as knitting. During the early centuries of Christianity the craft spread outwards from Arabia along the trade routes to Spain and later to the rest of Europe.

The Middle Ages

Evidence of any knitting activity recedes until the late Middle Ages. By the 14th and 15th centuries, with the influence of the Moorish conquests in Spain, the craft was firmly established there. Knitting had become more sophisticated: guilds in Spain (and Italy) were reknowned for their gifted craftsmen who made knitted items – gloves exist from this time – for religious and ceremonial occasions.

That knitting was firmly established in Europe by about 1400 is confirmed by the earliest known painting depicting knitting. It is by a German artist and shows the Virgin Mary at work with her needles.

15th and 16th centuries

The first references to knitting in the British Isles date back to the end of the 15th century during Tudor times. Then, there were a great many guilds with craftsmen producing woollen caps, gloves and stockings. The elasticity of knitting is perfect for covering and fitting the uneven shape of human limbs. During the reign of Elizabeth I silk stockings were highly-prized items of dress – by men (remember that they wore 'doublets and hose'). William Lee, a Nottinghamshire man, changed the face of knitting in 1589 when he invented a revolutionary frame for making stockings. The advances started by Lee were then carried on by his brother who established the frame knitting industry based around Nottingham and Leicester. It became an industry beleaguered by poor pay and oppressive labour relations.

Professional hand knitting survived only in regions which had strong knitting traditions – usually remote areas where it was imperative to have a secondary occupation (these included island groups to compensate when fishing and farming failed – in particular Shetland, Aran, and the Channel Islands, and also the Yorkshire Dales).

HISTORY

17th and 18th centuries

During the main part of this period the knitting trade continued to develop markets throughout Europe. There were always plenty of wars being fought and therefore a constant demand for stockings for the soldiers plus other items of army apparel. This was the 'golden age' of knitting: it was considered a necessary domestic skill for an accomplished woman.

Unfortunately the heyday of knitting could not last for ever – by the close of the 18th century an accumulation of circumstances brought about a decline in the industry. For hand knitters poor pay and materials meant that inferior goods were created: an abundance of framework knitters, in an industry where corrupt practises flourished, caused wages to drop and, finally when knee breeches and stockings were replaced by trousers, the knitting trade virtually collapsed.

○ During the late 19th century spinning and hand knitting was still carried out in many homes as a cottage industry.

The Industrial Revolution

After many years of adversity, an amazing change took place – the industrial revolution began creating new wealth for the flourishing middle classes. As leisure time became available to an increasing number of women, then knitting started to become accepted as a leisure pastime, along with embroidery, crochet and many other handicrafts.

Techniques had been passed on by word of mouth for generations, but by the 1840s publications with techniques and patterns began to appear. Many items were very intricate and even frivolous; we would not consider making them today.

The 20th century

After World War I, dress styles changed, becoming less formal and knitted garments as we know them today came into being. The 20s through to the outbreak of World War II saw a big revival in hand knitting with even Paris courturiers producing high fashion garments.

After the war the enthusiasm for knitting was curtailed by clothes rationing. Suddenly it was no longer smart to wear hand knits – knitting was banished to a homespun activity. Although it is often stated that in periods of depression it is cheaper to knit than to buy and therefore knitting becomes more popular at such times, in practice a revival of interest in knitting usually means that the fashion climate is congenial to it.

It was not until the 1970s that young designers began to be aware of the potential of knitting. A resurgence of interest in natural fibres and other new, exciting yarn developments, coupled with renewed awareness of the natural environment plus a passion for nostalgia provided exactly the right background for knitting to become the popular and creative pastime that it is today.

Styles from the 1950s

Basic Techniques

To produce any form of knitting you must master the basics of casting on (the method of evolving a foundation row of loops on to a needle so that knitting can commence), forming knit and purl stitches, and casting off (securing the stitches at the end of a piece of work). Although you may be fumble-fingered at first, you will be amazed at what you can achieve once these few simple techniques become second nature.

There are numerous versions of certain techniques, including casting on and off. Different techniques of casting on are used for various purposes, such as for elasticity, strength or decoration. Too many choices can prove confusing, particularly for a beginner, so in this book only the two most general-purpose methods using two needles or the thumb are described in the following pages: most knitters will find them more than adequate for a lifetime of knitting.

Similarly with casting off, the method shown on p.49 is the most popular, but it is only one of a number of methods. Alternative methods of casting on or off are explained for techniques where they may be preferable.

Holding the Needles and Yarn

If you are right-handed, hold the needle with the stitches in your left hand, and the needle with which you make the stitches in your right hand, as though you were holding a pencil. Your method of holding the yarn will develop as you practise knitting: there is no right way or wrong way, as long as you are relaxed it is a case of personal preference. If you are in doubt try the method shown here. It helps to control the yarn by winding it round the fingers of your right hand so that it flows evenly to make a fabric with firm, even tension. Use your index finger to wind the yarn round the needle.

If you are left-handed see pp.46–7.

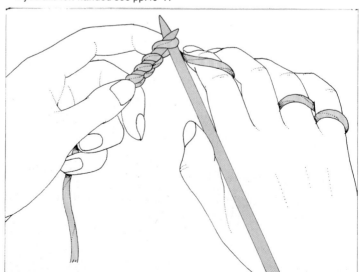

Making a Slip Knot

A slip knot forms the basis of casting on.

1 Leaving at least a 15cm (6in) length, make a loose knot in the end of the ball of yarn as shown.

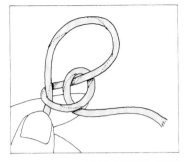

2 Take a needle in your right hand and insert it into the large loop at the top of the knot.

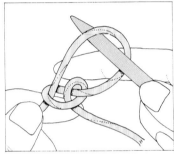

3 Pull both ends of yarn gently (one end in each hand) to tighten the knot on the needle. This is now your first cast-on stitch.

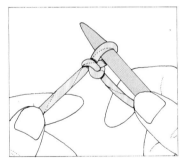

Tips

○ Beginners tend to knit loosely, but with practise you can control this tendency.

○ Some types of yarn needles are more suited to particular methods of casting on.

○ For making a slip knot and casting on, hold the needle in your right hand as though you are holding a pen.

Casting On – Two-Needle Cable Method

Use this method to give a neat, firm edge with a cabled appearance that is suitable for ribbing or other firm fabrics. It is not recommended for chunky yarns and it would be too heavy for cotton and other types of yarn without elasticity.

1 Hold the needle with the slip knot in your left hand. Insert the right-hand needle into the slip knot; wind the yarn over the top of the right-hand needle point and down between the two needles.

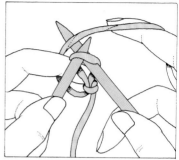

2 Use the right-hand needle point to pull a loop through the slip knot.

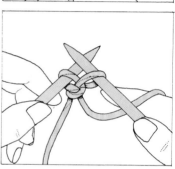

3 Transfer this new loop to the left-hand needle.

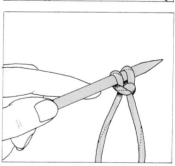

4 Work continues *between* the stitches rather than *into* them. Insert the right-hand needle point between the slip knot and the new stitch and wind the yarn over the right-hand needle point.

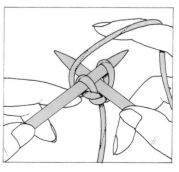

5 Pull a new loop through between the two stitches and transfer it to the left-hand needle. Continue in this way, always working between the last two stitches on the left-hand needle, for the number of stitches required.

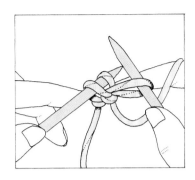

Casting On – Thumb Method

Only one needle is required – the left thumb acts as the second needle. The resulting edge is more elastic than the cable method, so it is ideal for using with stocking stitch or garter stitch fabrics.

1 Make a slip knot some distance from the end of the yarn (about one metre – this length must be sufficient to make all the cast-on stitches) and place it on the needle. Hold the needle in your right hand and wind the yarn from the ball round your left thumb as shown.

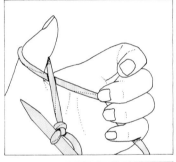

2 Insert the needle into the loop on your thumb. Using the length of yarn from the end of the ball (held in your right hand), wind it under and over the top of the needle.

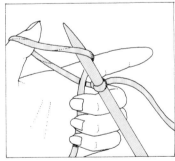

3 Draw a loop through and tighten it on the needle. Continue in this way until all the stitches have been cast on.

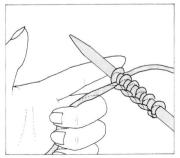

How to Knit

Mastering the knit stitch is vital: it is the most important stitch in knitting. At first your hands will be unfamiliar with the movements, but keep the flow of stitches even by sliding them up the left-hand needle so they are ready to be worked (watch that they do not fall off the end). Develop a style of holding the yarn and right-hand needle so that when you are working your right hand never loses contact with the needle. Try supporting the right-hand needle with your thumb under it; control the yarn with your index finger, which should be able to move sufficiently to wind the yarn round the needle tip.

If you are left-handed you may find this method unwieldy. If so, follow the instructions on p.47.

1 Hold the needle with the cast-on stitches in your left hand and the free needle in your right hand. Insert the right-hand needle from front to back into the first stitch.

2 With the yarn at the back of the work throughout, wind it under and over the top of the right-hand needle point in a clockwise direction.

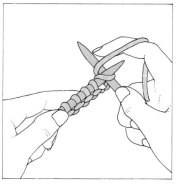

3 Draw the yarn through the stitch on the left-hand needle, so making a new stitch on the right-hand needle.

4 Slide the stitch just worked into from the left-hand needle, leaving the new stitch on the right-hand needle.

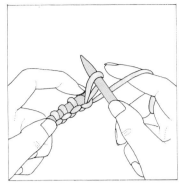

5 Work into each of the cast-on stitches in the same way until all the stitches are on the right-hand needle. To knit another row transfer the needle with the stitches to your left hand.

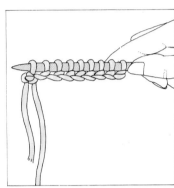

How to Purl

The second most important stitch in knitting, the purl stitch is used in conjunction with the knit stitch to make most fabrics.

An alternative method, suitable for left-handed knitters, is shown on p.47.

1 Hold the needle with the cast-on stitches in your left hand and the free needle in your right hand. Insert the right-hand needle from right to left into the *front* of the first stitch.

continued

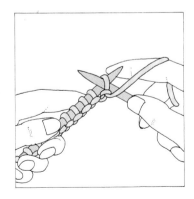

2 Keeping the yarn at the front of the work throughout, wind it over the top and round the right-hand needle in an anti-clockwise direction.

3 Draw the yarn through the stitch on the left-hand needle so making a new stitch on the right-hand needle.

4 Drop the stitch just worked from the left-hand needle. Work into each stitch to be purled in the same way. At the end of the row transfer the needle with the stitches to your left hand, ready to start the next row.

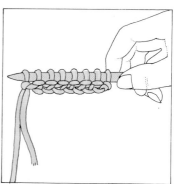

Guide for Left-Handed Knitters

Learning new manual skills and following diagrams that depict right-handed techniques is especially confusing if you are left-handed. In order to cast on and form the basic stitches you can simply reverse the diagrams by propping the book in front of a mirror and following the mirror image. Although in this case the yarn must be controlled by the left hand rather than the right, it is unnecessary and potentially complicated to reverse all the procedures – in particular rows should still be worked from right to left.

Knitting by the continental method is often the solution for left-handed knitters. Here the left hand holds the yarn while the needle is manipulated around it to form the stitch (normally the yarn is held in the right hand and wrapped around the needle to make a stitch).

How to knit – continental style

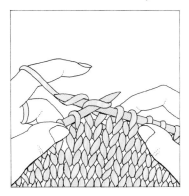 

1 Hold the yarn in your left hand with it looped round the index finger. Insert the right-hand needle from front to back into the stitch to be knitted, then twist it under the working strand of yarn from the index finger.

2 Use the right-hand needle to draw a new stitch through, then drop the loop from the left-hand needle in the usual way.

How to purl – continental style

 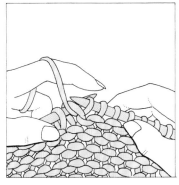

1 Holding the yarn in your left hand and keeping your index finger to the right of where you are working (behind the needles), insert the right-hand needle from back to front through the stitch to be purled.

2 Bring the working yarn forward slightly, then twist the right-hand needle from left to right around the yarn. Draw a new stitch through and drop the loop from the left-hand needle.

Joining in a New Ball of Yarn

It is almost impossible to complete a piece of knitting of any size without using more than one ball of yarn. The best place to join in a new ball of yarn is at the start of a row. If there is any doubt whether you have sufficient yarn to work another row, measure the remaining length across the work laid flat; you need about four times the width to complete a row.

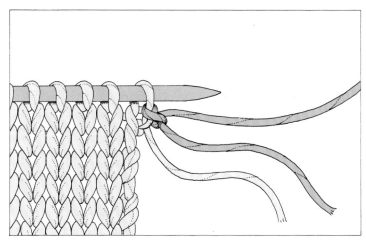

1 Leaving a sufficiently long end to darn in, attach the new yarn to the first stitch with a simple knot.

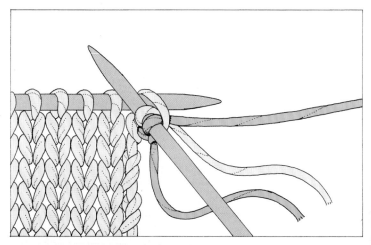

2 Further secure the join by working the first stitch with two ends of yarn – one from the new ball and the tail end of the old yarn. Drop the old yarn and continue working with the new yarn. Darn in the ends later (see p.174).

Casting Off

Casting off is a method of securing stitches at the end of a piece of work so that they do not unravel. The most common fault is a tight edge that puckers the fabric. Ideally the cast-off edge should have the same tension and elasticity as the rest of the fabric. Achieve this by casting off in the same stitch that you are working – if it is stocking stitch it is usual to cast off on a knit row.

1 Knit the first two stitches in the usual way so transferring them to the right-hand needle.

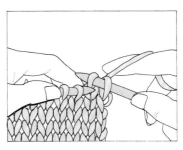

2 Use the left-hand needle point to lift the first stitch knitted over the second and off the needle.

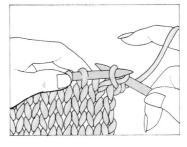

3 Knit another stitch on to the right-hand needle and repeat the process until one stitch remains. Cut the yarn, leaving a long length for seaming. Lengthen the remaining loop, then draw the cut end through and pull the yarn to tighten the stitch.

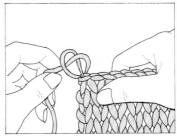

Tips

○ Leave at least a 15cm (6in) length of yarn when casting on – it can be used for seaming.

○ When learning to knit, speed is not important. Instead, try to achieve a relaxed style.

○ If your yarn runs out in the middle of a row, avoid joining new yarn at that point by taking the stitches back to the beginning of the row.

○ Avoid a too tight edge when casting off by using a needle that is one size larger.

Basic Fabrics

Before embarking on any knitting project, put your knit and purl techniques to good use by practising some simple fabrics. The stitches shown here are used over and over again and really do form the basis of the bulk of knitting. You will be surprised at how easy some of these are.

Garter Stitch (g st)

The most basic knitted fabric, garter stitch is produced by knitting every row to make a thickish, flat piece of work. Both sides are identical and consist of horizontal ridges that equal two rows, so it is quite slow growing. As garter stitch does not curl up, it can be used for bands and borders.

Stocking Stitch (st st)

This is the most popular knitted stitch. Knit and purl rows are alternated to form a fabric that looks very different on both sides. It is smooth and flat with a series of interlocking 'V's on the knitted side (which is traditionally the right side), with slightly textured, horizontal ridges on the opposite side. Unfortunately flat, smooth fabrics do tend to curl and roll up at the edges and stocking stitch is no exception: it must be neatened with a band or hem.

Reverse Stocking Stitch (rev st st)

Although it is technically the wrong side of stocking stitch, the reverse side of the fabric can be used as a stitch in its own right where a more textured look is required. The ridged appearance should not be confused with garter stitch. Here, the ridges sit next to each other, but in garter stitch they are separated by a gap the width of one row.

Moss Stitch (moss st)

A combination of alternate single knit and purl stitches across a row produces a simple textured fabric that is also reversible. It differs from ribbing (see p.52) in that the stitches are not in vertical lines, they alternate on each row so that stitches knitted in the first row will also be knitted in the following row.

Over an *odd* number of stitches, work every row as follows: K1, * P1, K1, rep from * to end.

With an *even* number of stitches work as follows:

1st row * K1, P1, rep from * to end.

2nd row * P1, K1, rep from * to end.

Repeat these 2 rows to form pattern.

Ribbing

This technique is used for many stitch patterns, some of them quite complicated, but basic ribbing consists of an easy combination of knit and purl stitches. This time it makes a very different fabric – one that is very elastic, pulls the work in dramatically, is slow to work and takes a lot of yarn.

Despite its drawbacks, the 'concertina' effect of ribbing makes it an ideal finishing border: it is the most popular form of welt, cuff and neckband. Tension is difficult to control because of constantly moving the yarn backwards and forwards. As a guide the ribbing on a garment should pull in to about two-thirds of the width of the main section. You will soon establish a feel for the correct tension as you put the theory into practice.

Single Rib (K1, P1 rib)

Most often used for ribbed bands, single rib consists of alternating vertical lines of knit and purl stitches. To keep the lines unbroken, stitches that were knitted in one row must be purled in the following row, and vice versa. Ribbed bands are usually worked with needles two sizes smaller than the main fabric; if the tension varies smaller needles produce a tidier result.

Over an *even* number of stitches, work every row as follows: * K1, P1, rep from * to end.

With an *odd* number of stitches, work as follows:

1st row K1, * P1, K1, rep from * to end.
2nd row P1, * K1, P1, rep from * to end.

Tips

○ Master stocking stitch at an early stage; it is so well known that it is widely used for tension guidance.

○ When moving yarn to the back or front of the work for ribbed stitches, make sure that it goes between the needles. There is a tendency to take the yarn over the top of needles which results in extra stitches or strands.

Double Rib (K2, P2 rib)

A variation of single rib where the number of alternating knit and purl stitches is doubled. It makes a perfectly acceptable substitute for a ribbed band, although the 'pulling in' effect is less intense than with single rib. Usually worked over a multiple of four stitches, every row is as follows: * K2, P2, rep from * to end.

Rib Variations

Many basic rib fabrics are the result of combining varying numbers of knit and purl stitches – say, four knit stitches and one purl (below), or five purl stitches and two knit (bottom). The permutations are endless, but remember that the more stitches you have in one type before changing to the next will make a looser rib. Wide ribs do not have the same grip as single or double ones.

How to Decrease

Decreasing is a method of reducing stitches to shape a piece of knitted fabric. There are numerous methods of shaping, but simple (basic) shaping can be worked at any point in a row as well as at the edges. If a pattern states 'dec one st' without telling you exactly how, opt for knitting or purling two stitches together (K2 tog/P2 tog).

Basic Decreasing
K2 tog

1 Insert the right-hand needle from left to right through the front of the second stitch on the left-hand needle, then continue in the same way through the first stitch.

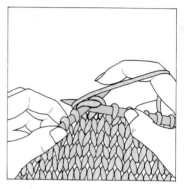

2 Continue as though knitting a stitch, drawing a new loop through the *two* stitches on the left-hand needle.

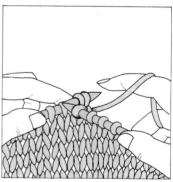

3 Drop the two knitted-together stitches off the left-hand needle, leaving a single stitch on the right-hand needle.

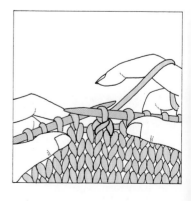

P2 tog

1 Insert the right-hand needle from right to left through the front of the two stitches being worked together.

2 Continue as though purling a stitch, drawing a new loop through the *two* stitches on the left-hand needle.

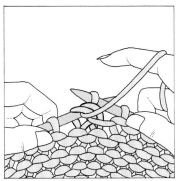

3 Drop the two purled-together stitches off the left-hand needle, leaving a single stitch on the right-hand needle.

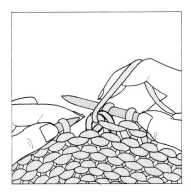

Tip

○ When shaping side edges, try decreasing one stitch in from the end to maintain a neater edge.

Paired Decreasing

All decreases slope either to the right or left. The basic method of working two stitches together always produces a slant to the right. For a finished piece of work to look professional the decreases should follow the line of shaping.

When both edges are being shaped, say for raglan armholes, there are pairs of decreases that work well together: it is best to work them two or three stitches in from the edge to form a neat-looking border and an edge that is ideal for sewing up.

There are many variations of paired decreasing. The method described here is the most frequently used and simple to work. Where alternative methods appear in a pattern they are usually given in full.

On right-side rows, K2 tog always slopes to the right: pair it with another method of decreasing – slip one, knit one, pass slipped stitch over (sl 1, K1, psso) that produces a slope to the left.

Sl 1, K1, psso

1 Work to the position of the decrease, then slip the next stitch from the left-hand needle to the right-hand one without working it. Knit the next stitch on the left-hand needle in the usual way.

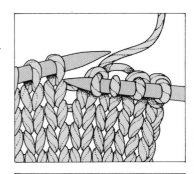

2 Use the left-hand needle point to lift the slipped stitch over the last stitch worked and off the right-hand needle – so decreasing one stitch.

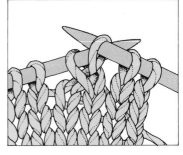

A gentle slope forms when the decreasing only occurs on right-side rows using 'sl 1, K1, psso' at the beginning of a row (within a border of two stitches) and K2 tog at the end.

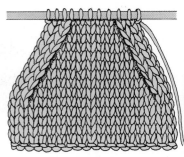

Tips

○ When slipping stitches in decreasing, assume that all knit stitches are slipped knitwise and all purl stitches purlwise, unless specified otherwise.

○ Work shaped edges loosely, taking care that they do not pull.

On wrong-side rows, P2 tog slopes to the right when viewed from the right side of the work: pair it with 'purl two together through back of loops' (P2 tog tbl) to make a slant to the left.

P2 tog tbl

1 Work to the position of the decrease, then insert the right-hand needle from left to right through the *back* of the next two stitches on the left-hand needle.

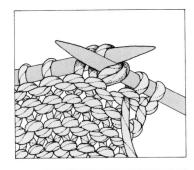

2 Purl in the usual way, drawing one loop only through the two stitches, so decreasing one stitch.

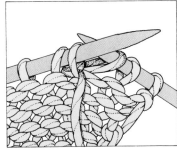

A steep slope requires shaping on every row rather than the alternate rows of a gentle slope. Work the decreases on the right side as before (sl 1, K1, psso at the beginning and K2 tog at the end); for the wrong-side rows use P2 tog at the beginning of a row and P2 tog tbl at the end.

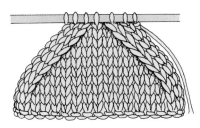

How to Increase

Shaping a fabric to make it wider is called increasing. There are various methods of gaining extra stitches, but making two stitches out of one (increase one stitch – inc one st/inc 1) is the simplest and most popular. It can be applied to both knit and purl stitches and worked anywhere in the row. An alternative basic method of making a stitch (make one st/M1) involves working into a raised strand of yarn from between the needles.

Basic Increasing – inc one st/inc 1

To increase in a *knit* stitch, first work into the front and then into the back of the same stitch.

1 Knit a stitch in the usual way, making a new loop on the right-hand needle, but do not drop the original loop from the left-hand needle.

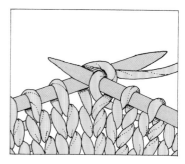

2 Twist the right-hand needle point until it lies behind the left-hand one. Insert the right-hand needle from right to left into the back of the original stitch remaining on the left-hand needle; knit into this in the usual way allowing the original stitch to drop from the left-hand needle.

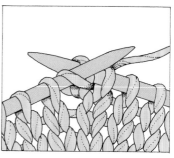

This type of increase is slightly visible. On the right side of the work you will notice a horizontal bar across the line of stitches.

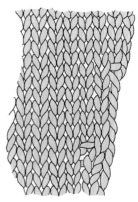

To increase into a *purl* stitch also requires working into the front and back of the same stitch.

1 Purl a stitch in the usual way without dropping the original loop from the left-hand needle.

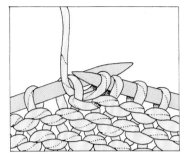

2 Twist the right-hand needle-point behind the left one and insert it from left to right into the back of the original stitch (this looks a very awkward move, but it is correct). Now purl as usual allowing the original loop to fall from the left-hand needle.

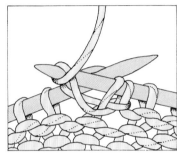

Making a Stitch – make one st/M1

1 Work to the position of the increase. Use the tip of the right-hand needle to lift the top horizontal strand lying between the needles and place it on the left-hand needle.

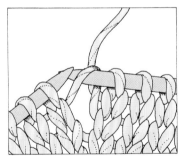

2 Make a new stitch by knitting the lifted strand through the back of the loop to prevent a small hole forming.

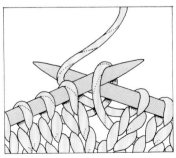

Selvedges

The side edges of a piece of knitting are called 'selvedges', as with a length of fabric. Specific methods of making a neat selvedge are seldom referred to in a pattern. The basic techniques are very simple to work and easy to incorporate into your knitting. It is best to plan ahead and choose an edge according to the type of fabric and the ultimate use of the edge.

Basic Neatness
Garter stitch fabric

Garter stitch knitted without special neatening selvedges often tends to be untidy due to the adjustment of tension at the beginning of the rows. To avoid this, work as follows.

1st row Slip first stitch purlwise, take the yarn to the back between the needles, knit to end.

Repeat this row to produce selvedges with a neat chain effect.

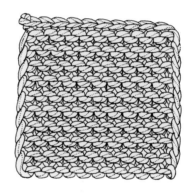

Stocking stitch fabric

The side edges of stocking stitch should be firm, without being too tight (the stitches will break) or too loose (the edge becomes wavy and does not hold the fabric in shape).

Work in the usual way without any undue stretching of the edge stitches. To knit, or purl, the first stitch of a row as tightly as possible, insert only the tip of the needle into the edge stitch.

Edge to be Picked Up

Some side edges of a fabric are used later for picking up stitches to accommodate a band or border, such as the button/buttonhole bands on a cardigan or jacket. The selvedges shown here form a larger-than-normal stitch at the ends of rows which is easy to see and use later for picking up stitches.

Garter stitch fabric
Use the chain effect edge as described above for basic neatness.

Stocking stitch fabric

Simply slip the first stitch on every row, then proceed to the end of the row as usual. The slipped stitch is extended over two rows, so enlarging it, before being worked again.

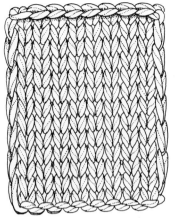

For Seaming

Garter stitch fabric

This fabric knitted in the usual way makes an edge that is ideal for seaming. The 'chain' selvedge described for neatness is too loopy for this situation.

Stocking stitch fabric

1st row K to end.
2nd row K1, P to end.

Repeat these two rows to form a selvedge with a neat, 'pipped' effect created by the knitted stitches at the beginning and end of every row. The 'pips' are an ideal guide for sewing up a flat seam (see p.176).

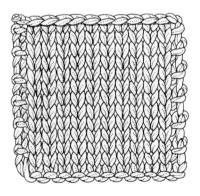

Tip

○ Unless otherwise stated, remember that knit stitches should be slipped knitwise and purl stitches slipped purlwise.

Picking Up Stitches

Many garments have sections, such as neckbands, borders or collars, that are added after the main part is finished. They are incorporated into the main piece of work – rather than made separately and sewn on afterwards – by a process called 'picking (or knitting) up stitches'. The name implies that loops are merely caught up from the edge of a fabric; in reality 'pick up and knit' is a more accurate term to describe the action of using a ball of yarn to make an entirely new row of loops. It is essential to enclose the edge that you are picking up from in order to neaten it and avoid unsightly holes.

Deciding Which Stitches to Pick Up

Most patterns stipulate the exact number of stitches to be picked up along an edge. The number depends on whether the stitches are picked up along a row or down a line, and the tension of the stitch used for working the knitted up stitches. In general, cast-off or held stitches are used stitch for stitch; for an edge, where the row tension is greater than the stitch tension, about one row in four is missed in the picking up. It is important to distribute the stitches being picked up evenly along the edge. Fold the edge into half and mark this point with a pin; repeat with markers at the quarter-way (and eighth-way) points, depending on the length of the edge. Now divide the total number of stitches equally and concentrate on picking up that number from each section.

How to Pick Up Stitches

There are a number of popular ways of picking up stitches: choose the one that you are most comfortable with. Whichever method you prefer, use a knitting needle – or crochet hook – one or two sizes smaller than recommended in the pattern to avoid stretching the edge stitches. You can revert to the correct size needles for the actual knitting.

Unless instructed otherwise, you should pick up stitches with the right side of the work facing you and working in a right to left direction.

Method 1 – using a knitting needle

Hold the needle in your right hand and support the section of edge to be worked on between the thumb and forefinger of your left hand. Insert the needle into the edge, wind the yarn round the needle as though knitting a stitch and draw a loop through. Continue in this way along the edge until you have the required number of loops. Left-handed knitters can use this technique working in reverse.

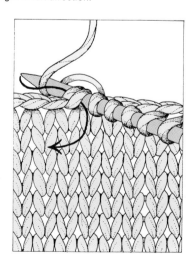

Method 2 – using a crochet hook (quick and efficient for right-handed knitters)

1 Hold the hook in your right hand and support the edge as given for Method 1 (opposite). Insert the hook from front to back through the edge, wind the yarn round the hook and draw through a loop.

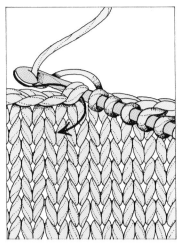

2 Continue in this way until the hook is full of stitches, then slip them off the back of the hook on to a needle.

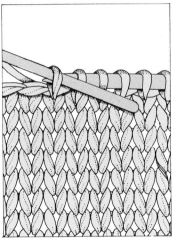

Method 3 – using a crochet hook (suitable for left-handed knitters)

Holding the hook in your left hand, insert it from front to back through the edge. Wind the yarn round the hook and draw a loop through. Place the loop on to a needle held in the right hand.

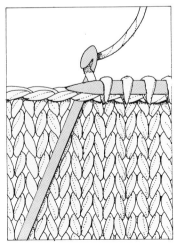

Types of Edge

The following examples show the main situations for picking up stitches that you are likely to encounter. Each requires extra detail or slight modifications to the technique described on pp.62–3.

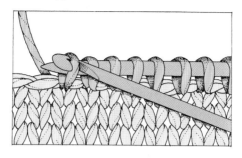

Cast-on or cast-off/horizontal edge

The cast-off base for picked-up stitches should be fairly loose: use a size larger needle for casting off in this situation. Always draw a new stitch through both loops of the chain edge – one loop is not strong enough and can leave a ridged effect on the right side of the work. Pick up stitch for stitch unless otherwise directed in the instructions.

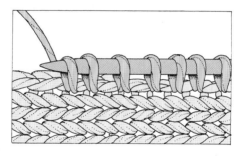

Side or vertical edge

Ideally the fabric should have a chain selvedge (see p.62) as a base for picking up stitches. Each chain at the side covers two rows. It is usually not sufficient to knit up from under the two loops of each chain; you will also have to knit up stitches from the point where the two chains overlap. Note the effect on the wrong side of the work – the original chain edge remains intact as a flat ridge.

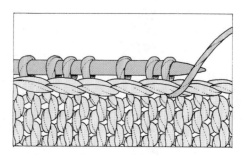

If there is no special selvedge, always pick up a new stitch from under two loops to make a firm base. It should be easy to keep the work straight by following a line of stitches.

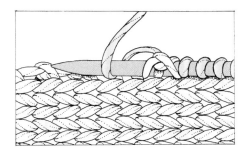

Shaped/diagonal edge
Sometimes shaping, say for a V neckline, is arranged two or three stitches in from the edge. Often it forms a decorative feature, but it also gives a cleaner line for picking up stitches. Follow the guidelines for picking up stitches from a side or vertical edge.

Edge incorporating 'held' stitches
When picking up stitches from a neckline for instance, it is quite common to find a section of edge that contains 'held' stitches (those retained on a holder) often between two areas of stitches to be picked up. Before reaching the held section, knit up stitches as usual, then prevent a hole forming by picking up another stitch from the loop separating the knitted-up stitches and those on the holder (do this again at the end of the held stitches); do not cut off the yarn. Slip the held stitches on to the spare needle and, using the needle with the picked-up stitches, knit across them. Continue to pick up stitches as required.

Tips

○ Avoid holes – you can see a hole forming as you insert the needle. If this happens, try a different stitch.

○ If the edge has stretched, first sew a contrast, slippery yarn (so that it can easily be removed) around the edge and draw it up to the correct size. The contrast yarn can be pulled out after a few rows.

○ Never start work on an edge (unless it is very short) just picking up stitches as you go along. The chances of reaching the correct number of stitches by the end of the edge, or achieving an even distribution, are very small.

○ If the knitting up line is untidy you can disguise it with a slightly decorative ridge by knitting a row if it is the wrong side of the fabric (or purling a right-side row) before continuing with the appropriate stitch and needle size.

Bands and Borders

Bands or borders are alternative names used to describe the same part of a knitted garment (to save confusion from here on they are referred to as bands). A band is a section worked in a flat fabric to counteract the curling tendencies of a knitted fabric – both cast-on and cast-off edges, as well as side edges, will roll if left to their own devices.

Rib, moss stitch and garter stitch are the three flat fabrics closely associated with bands, which are usually worked with smaller needles than the original fabric to encourage neatness.

Usually bands are picked up and knitted on to an edge, or worked separately and sewn on afterwards. They can also be knitted in with the main fabric, but this method is seldom used as problems can arise in controlling two tensions within a single row of knitting.

Picked-up Bands

This type of band is mainly used for neckbands and armbands. It is worked from picked-up stitches (see p.62) and is most likely to be in rib for maximum elasticity. As the band is meant to control the edge, the calculation of the number of stitches picked up is important – the band must be on the tight side, yet without being so tight that it puckers the main fabric or so loose that it frills.

Usually one seam is left open – one shoulder for the neckband or the side seam for an armband – and the band is worked flat using two needles. To avoid seams altogether it is possible to work in rounds with a set of double-ended needles. Choose the method that suits you best. The general format for a band in this situation is to work to the required depth and then cast off, usually in rib.

Top with 'picked-up' neckband
and armbands

Jacket with separate front bands

Separate Bands

These are narrow strips of a flat fabric – usually rib – worked separately and sewn on afterwards. They are often used as button and buttonhole bands for cardigans and jackets.

Apart from neatness, the emphasis is on careful fitting of the band. A specific measurement is not usually quoted, so length is a question of fitting to the edge as you go along. Every so often, while still on the needles, the band should be slightly stretched and then pinned to the edge until it fits the entire length.

There are a number of variations in style and method that you might encounter. The jacket with a collar has button and buttonhole bands worked entirely independently. Make the button band first and sew it in place. The positions of the buttons can be marked with pins so that they are evenly spaced. Finally the buttonhole band is knitted and measured against the button band so that the buttonholes are made in the correct place, matching the pinned positions (see pp.70–3 for buttonholes).

Where the welts (and sometimes neckbands) are in the same stitch, it is feasible to cast on all the stitches (for the welt plus front band) together. When the welt is complete, the band stitches are left on a safety-pin and returned to once the remainder of the front is finished. The front band is then knitted separately, fitting as before, until the neck shaping is reached and then it is cast off; or if the neckband is in the same stitch, the neckband stitches can be incorporated into it without further seaming.

A band can also be made in one continuous section that fits up one front, round the back neck and down the other front. Quite often this type of band is made in two sections with a seam joining them at the centre back neck to make alterations easier.

As the front bands are a focal point of a garment, take great care when sewing them in place – always pin in position first and use a flat seam (see p.176) for attaching them.

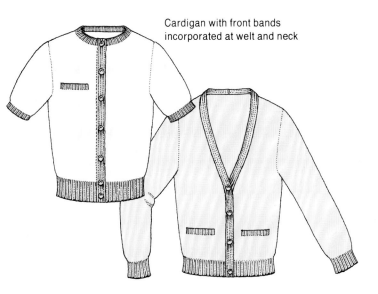

Cardigan with front bands
incorporated at welt and neck

Cardigan with bands worked
in two sections

Tubular Casting Off

Instead of folding a ribbed neckband in half (basically to disguise the often unruly cast-off edge) which takes time and makes a double fabric, try tubular casting off. It has a similar neat appearance to the folded edge and this accounts for its alternative name of 'invisible' casting off. Also use it for any other close-fitting necklines such as polo necks. Work loosely to keep the edge elastic so allowing it to pull easily over the head. Cut the yarn (this end is used for casting off) so that it is at least four times the width of the edge to be cast off. Thread the cut yarn into a blunt-ended sewing needle.

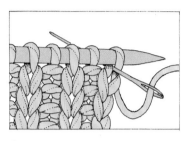

1 Starting with a knit stitch, insert the sewing needle knitwise into the first stitch and slip it off the left-hand needle.

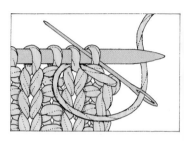

2 Miss the following purl stitch and insert the sewing needle purlwise through the next knit stitch; draw the yarn through. Now, thread the yarn purlwise through the missed purl stitch and slip it off the needle.

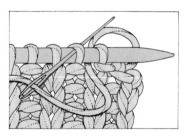

3 Insert the sewing needle from back to front *between* the first and second stitches; draw the yarn through to the front. Insert the sewing needle knitwise through the next purl stitch and draw the yarn through.

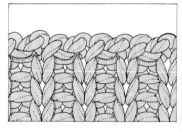

4 Repeat steps 1 to 3. Once you become familiar with working this method it is a quick and easy way of making a neat and elastic finish.

Tip

○ Allow for a ribbed band stretching widthways and becoming shallower once it has been cast off. If the band looks the correct depth on the needle, add a couple more rows to be sure.

Sewing in a Zip Fastener

Instead of using buttons for fastening, an open-ended zip fastener may be incorporated into front bands. Ordinary, closed zips are also useful for back neck openings (especially on children's sweaters for extra room when pulling them on) and skirt side or back seams.

You can use standard dressmaking zips, but remember to match the weight of the zip to that of the fabric – knitted fabrics are often heavier than those used for sewing. The finished zip should open easily without catching any knitted edge; if it does, you have stitched too close to the teeth. Match the length of the opening and that of the zip exactly. A zip that is too short will make the seam bulge, while one that is too long will drag the sides of the opening.

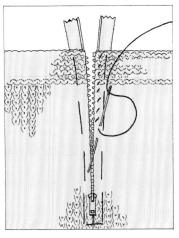 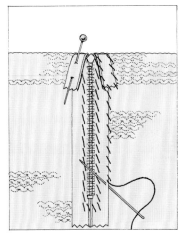

1 Working on the right side of the fabric, pin the zip into the opening with the ends of the tape extended, teeth facing upwards and level with the top of the opening. For fine fabrics the sides of the opening should meet so that the teeth are concealed: with thicker fabrics, such as those for outdoor wear, leave the teeth exposed. Tack along both sides of the zip using an ordinary sewing needle and thread.

2 Remove the pins. Thread a sewing needle to match the colour of the fabric. With the zip open, secure the thread at the top right-hand side of the zip. Make a stab stitch (which will be virtually invisible in the knitted pile) by bringing the needle through to the front and re-inserting it a minute distance to the right. Bring the needle through to the front again

about 5mm ($\frac{1}{4}$in) to the left of the previous stitch. Continue in this way, down the first side of the opening, working the stitches as close as possible to the edge of the work. For a back neck or skirt seam opening, work a few extra stitches across the bottom of the zip before continuing up the second side. It is easier to work the second side with the zip closed.

3 The back of the zip tape should also look neat. To finish off on the wrong side, fold the extended tapes back so that they are level with the top of the zip and angle them slightly to the side to avoid obstructing the zip slider; pin in position. Using a matching thread, keep the tapes in place by oversewing all round the outer edges, catching down the folded-back tapes in the same way.

Buttonholes

A buttonhole is a small, closed slit – either horizontal or vertical – used for fastening a button; it is often placed in a front band or border. Although it is merely a finishing detail, a sloppy, untidy buttonhole can mar an otherwise well-made garment.

The position and spacing of buttonholes is important. Usually a pattern stipulates where the top and lower buttonholes must be – not too near the edge, about 2–3cm (1in) away depending on the thickness of the yarn. The remainder of the buttonholes are 'spaced evenly between', but there is some licence in the way that you interpret this. You may want to put two buttons close together on a deep welt to control it, or use pairs of buttonholes, instead of single ones, throughout. For further inspiration study the arrangement of buttonholes on the clothes in your wardrobe.

There are various methods of making buttonholes. Those described here are the most popular and all provide a neat finish with no need of further stitching or reinforcement.

Eyelet Buttonhole

The simplest form of buttonhole is merely a small hole called an 'eyelet'. It is suitable only for fine yarns and small buttons – hence its traditional use in baby and toddler clothes.

1 Unless otherwise instructed, make the eyelet on a right-side row. Work to the position of the buttonhole, then, if the yarn is at the back of the work, bring it to the front between the needles and knit the next two stitches together.

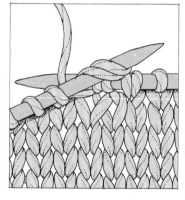

2 Work the next row in the usual way to complete the buttonhole. Although you have decreased a stitch in the previous row, the 'yarn over the needle' action compensates for it. When you reach the long loop created by the 'yarn over the needle' you must work into it in the usual way.

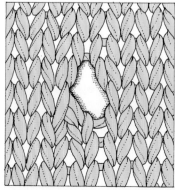

Horizontal Buttonholes

Basic

This popular buttonhole is worked over two rows, usually in a ribbed band. Keep the tension fairly tight when casting off to avoid over-stretching the hole.

1 On the first row (a right-side row) rib to the position of the buttonhole, then cast off the buttonhole stitches, working as usual in rib. (Remember that you must work *two* of the buttonhole stitches before you can begin casting off.) Rib to the end of the row.

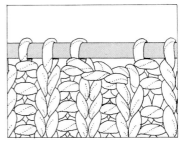

2 On the second row, rib to the cast-off stitches. To enable exactly the same number of cast-off stitches to be cast on by the two-needle method (see p.42), you must turn the work. Turn the work again to complete the row in rib.

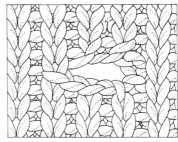

Tip

○ This type of buttonhole may be untidy, especially at the corners. For a neater version cast off one less stitch than required. Slip the last loop back on to the left-hand needle and (in rib) work it together with the next stitch. On the following row cast on one more stitch than required. After turning the work, slip the last cast-on stitch back on to the left-hand needle and rib it together with the next stitch.

Reinforced

This is a stronger, neater version of the basic method. It is worked over one row, therefore it can be tackled from either side of the work.

1 Rib to the position of the buttonhole. With the yarn in the correct position for working, slip the next stitch. Move the yarn into place for the following stitch and leave it there. Slip the next stitch; lift the first slipped stitch over the second, so casting it off without working it.

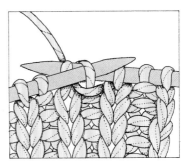

continued

2 Keeping the yarn in the correct place each time, cast off the required number of stitches in this way – by slipping them first. Transfer the loop remaining on the right-hand needle after the stitches have been cast off back to the left-hand needle.

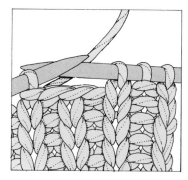

3 Turn the work round. Insert the right-hand needle *between* the last two stitches on the left-hand one and, using the cable method (see p.42) cast on the number of stitches cast off plus one extra.

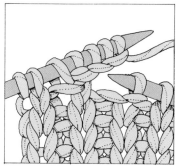

4 Turn the work again. Slip the last cast-on stitch on the right-hand needle to the left-hand needle and work it together with the next stitch on the needle. Rib to the end of the row.

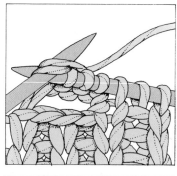

5 Continue across all stitches in rib as before. The finished buttonhole is less elastic than the basic horizontal buttonhole – therefore it is not as likely to stretch out of shape.

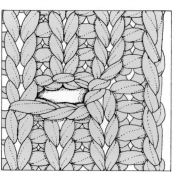

Vertical Buttonhole

You may require this less common buttonhole if a garment has a vertical pull. It is a simple method and requires no shaping other than dividing the work, then completing each half separately.

1 Work to the position of the buttonhole. Join in another ball of yarn to the stitches on the left-hand needle and continue to work each side separately with its respective ball of yarn.

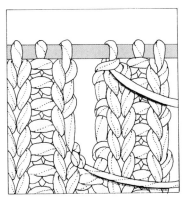

2 When the buttonhole is the required depth, close the gap by working across both sets of stitches with the first ball of yarn; cut off the second ball, leaving a long end. Continue as usual using one ball of yarn only. When darning in the cut ends at the top and lower edge of the buttonhole, use them to make strengthening stitches across the weak points at the corners.

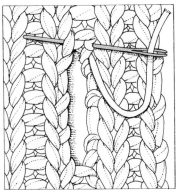

Tips

○ Check that there are at least three stitches between the edge of the fabric and the start of a buttonhole.

○ In ribbed bands, start and end horizontal buttonholes in purl stitches; also keep vertical buttonholes in a line of purl stitches.

○ As ribbing is so elastic, buttons will probably fit into a smaller hole than you imagine.

○ Choose your buttons first. It is easy to make a buttonhole to fit, but more difficult to find a button that is a suitable colour, style and size.

Necklines and Neckbands

The selection of necklines with their appropriate 'trims' (neckbands) shown here is standard styling for knitted garments. These neckbands are all methods of neatening a neck that has no other form of opening, by picking up stitches from the main fabric and working directly on to it – see the details on pp.62–5 for an explanation of basic techniques.

If you are following a printed pattern, details of working the neck shaping are usually described in full. However, if you understand how a neckline is achieved, depending on your skill and confidence, you may be able to adapt a pattern – substituting one neckline for another. There is even scope for a knitter with limited skills to create an individual touch by choosing a different neckband, or maybe a collar (see pp.78–81).

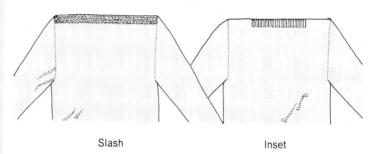

Slash   Inset

Slash Neck

This is the most basic of necklines. It is a straight line from shoulder to shoulder without any shaping. When sewing up the garment you merely leave a gap in the centre that is wide enough to pull over the head without it being so wide that it then slips off the shoulder.

If the fabric is one that curls, such as stocking stitch, it will need finishing at the cast-off edge to prevent it rolling at the neck. You can work a few extra rows and turn them to the wrong side to form a facing. Alternatively, work a few rows in a non-curling stitch, such as garter stitch or moss stitch, before casting off; this will give a yoke effect. The third method is strictly more correct, but involves a bit more planning.

Inset Neckband

The ribbed trim at the neck here complements the ribbing at the welt and cuffs: it is set into the body of the garment so that the shoulders and neck still form a continuous straight line.

To plan an inset neckband, you must calculate how many stitches there will be in it. Work on the basis that the gap required for an average adult head is 20cm (8in). Complete the front or back of the garment to a depth of 3cm (1¼in) less than the finished length. As the ribbing at the centre must be worked on smaller needles than the main fabric (to match the ribbing elsewhere), divide the work at this point, leaving the neck stitches on a holder. After finishing each side of the neck separately, return to the stitches on the holder and, using smaller needles, work 3cm (1¼in) in rib. Cast off in rib. Join each side of the neckband to the main fabric with a flat seam (see p.176), making extra stitches for strength at the corners of the neck on the top edge.

Crew Neck

This popular, traditional neckline should resemble a semi-circular shape (hence its alternative name – 'round' neck) when it is viewed from the front. The exact shaping depends on the depth of the neck (the measurement from the start of the shoulder shaping to its lowest point at the centre front) – usually about 7cm (2¾in) on an adult garment. At the point where the shaping commences on the front, the work is divided and a number of stitches at the centre front are left on a holder. Each side of the neck is then completed separately.

Further shaping, in the form of decreases at the neck edge, is required to form a semi-circle meeting up with the inner edge of the shoulder. Ideally the number of rows in the neck should be divided into three – the lower portion should have decreases at the neck on every row, the middle section on every alternate row, and the top portion should be straight with no decreases.

Back neck shaping often takes the form of a slight indentation following the curve of the front. Often it is only about four rows deep. Again the work is divided

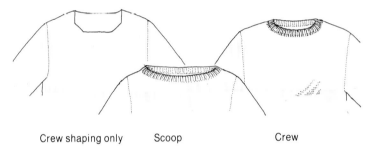

Crew shaping only   Scoop   Crew

leaving the back neck stitches (minus a few) on a holder. The remaining extra stitches are then decreased at the neck on every row so that the shoulders match up. Frequently, though, back neck shaping is overlooked and, once the shoulder shaping is complete, the remaining stitches that form the back neck are left on a holder.

This type of neckline has such deep curves that it is too steep to be finished with a flat fabric, such as garter or moss stitch. Instead it requires a ribbed neckband that needs no shaping. It is knitted directly onto the fabric, with stitches picked up from the edge. Before picking up stitches (see p.62), join the right shoulder seam so that you start work (with the right side facing you) at the left shoulder and continue down the front neck. To avoid a seam in the neckband it is possible to join both shoulder seams, then use a set of four needles to pick up and work the neckband.

A crew neckband is usually about 3cm (1¼in) deep: you must always cast off in rib, keeping your tension loose. For a neater finish you can work a double neckband by knitting double the length of the finished neckband plus an extra row for turning, then cast off very loosely. After joining the neckband seam, fold it in half to the wrong side and slip stitch the band in place along the row at the base. A tubular cast-off edge (see p.68) gives a similar appearance without the bulk of a double fabric.

Scoop Neck

Often mistaken for a crew neckline because of the similarity in shape and finish, a scoop (or 'boat') neckline is wider and flatter than a crew neck. With its more open look, it is a popular style for summer garments. The front neck shaping is often repeated on the back so that the back and front are alike.

V Neck

This is another classic neckline that will be familiar to everybody, and is often used on school and sports sweaters. The depth of the base of the V is variable as it is much easier to shape a V neckband to make it fit. Normally shaping for the neckline begins at around the same point as the underarms – about 20cm (8in) down from the shoulders on an average woman's garment and 25cm (10in) on a man's. The front of the garment is divided in half at the centre. If there is an odd number of stitches, the centre one is left on a safety pin and later forms the centre stitch at the axis of the neckband. Where the work splits into two even halves, a centre stitch is made by picking up and knitting a stitch from the horizontal loop lying between the two sets of stitches.

Each side of the neck is completed separately. The stitches at the neck edge are gradually and evenly decreased until they are in line with the edge of the shoulder. Shaping should be completed about 4cm (1¼in) from the shoulder to allow for a few straight rows to sit along the side of the neck.

A ribbed neckband, consisting of stitches picked up from the edge, usually neatens the neckline. The band is shaped by decreasing at both sides of the centre stitch – which is kept in stocking stitch throughout – at the point of the V. Depending on the angle of the V you may have to decrease on every row if it is very steep, or on alternate rows for a wider angle. Keep the rib correct throughout the shapings and cast off in rib, working the shapings as usual.

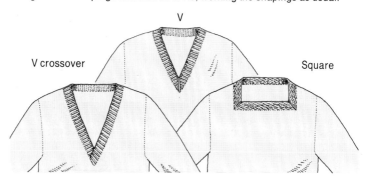

V

V crossover

Square

Crossover Neckband

A variation of the shaped, ribbed neckband, this style is worked in two sections that overlap at the centre front as there is no shaping to deal with the fullness. After joining one shoulder seam, the first section comprises stitches picked up down one side of the front neck. The second section goes from the point of the V, up the other side of the front neck and across the back neck. Each section is worked independently, without shaping, and then cast off in rib.

After overlapping the bands, the side edges are slip stitched in position along the angle of the neckline on both the front and back of the garment, so forming a diamond effect at the point of the V.

Square Neck

Square necklines are simple to work as they require a minimum of shaping. You work to the position of the base of the neckline – this can be any depth that you require – and then divide the work, leaving the centre front or back neck stitches on a holder or spare needle. Each side of the neck is then knitted separately by working straight to the shoulder.

Making a neat neckband is more of a problem for a square neck because of the right-angled corners, which must be mitred. Frequently neckbands are worked in garter stitch, rather than in rib, as it is easy and provides a neat finish. The easiest method of working a band involves knitting the central garter stitch rows in one with the main fabric; these rows form the base of the band. When the band is the required depth, cast off the stitches in the centre, leaving some in garter stitch at either end on safety pins. (The held stitches will form the side edges of the band – they should be equal in width to the depth of the base.)

If the back of the garment also has a square neck, cast off all the band stitches once it has been completed (leaving no stitches on pins). After the back and front are finished, join them at the shoulder seams. Rejoin the yarn (see p.48) to one set of stitches held on a safety pin and continue in garter stitch until the band fits along the sides of the neck reaching the top of the other band (below right).

Mitred Corners

When the bands that fit along the base of the neck and those that fit up the sides are worked simultaneously, the corners must be mitred so that the stitches lie at right angles to one another, divided by a central axis (below left).

To work a band with mitred corners, pick up stitches down the sides and along the base of the neck, making an extra stitch in the corner to form the axis. Place a marker at either side of the axis stitches and keep them in stocking stitch throughout. Work until the band is the required depth, decreasing one stitch at each side of the axis stitches on alternate rows.

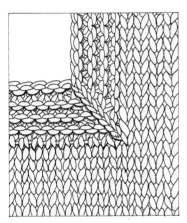
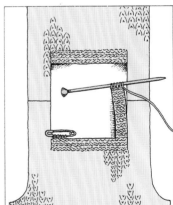

Tips

○ Cast off a crew neckband in rib using a needle one or two sizes larger to keep the edge loose and flexible.

○ Because of the depth of the opening there are usually a lot of stitches in a V neckband. If there are too many to cope with comfortably on two needles, transfer them to a circular needle and work backwards and forwards in rows.

○ When picking up stitches for a V neckband, slip a marker on to the needles at either side of the centre stitch – they will help you identify the stitch on subsequent rows.

Collars

Adding, or changing, a knitted collar is one of the easiest ways of giving sweaters, cardigans or jackets an individual look, or just revamping a favourite garment. The scope for different designs is endless; as well as varying the collar style or shape, the same collar will look completely different on garments with necklines of varying depths.

Most collars are worked in a flat fabric – usually rib for flexibility in fitting and to prevent them curling. They may be knitted directly on to the garment with stitches that have been picked up from the neckline (like an extended neckband), although frequently they are made separately and sewn on afterwards. For separate collars the cast-on edge should fit the neckline with the cast-off row forming the outer edge. Unless otherwise specified, sew the collar in position using a flat seam (see p.176).

The collars shown here are just a few of the basic shapes, with details of how to achieve them. Some collars are more suited to certain necklines: crew or round neck – straight, polo collars; scoop neck – cowl collar; V neck – shaped shawl collar; square neck – straight shawl, sailor collars.

Straight Collar

When it is worked separately this type of collar is a long, straight strip up to 7cm (2¾in) in depth. It is particularly suitable for a round neck; indeed, you can work a straight collar directly on to a crew neckband as an extension of it. This is simplest to do if you are working the neckband in the round with a circular needle – after about 1.5cm (½in) split the work at the centre front and continue in rows rather than rounds.

For a separate collar that is deeper than 7cm (2¾in) it is best to widen it towards the outer edge so that it will sit neatly on the shoulders. Cast on stitches for the neck edge using the same size needles as those used for the welt and cuffs, then work a few centimetres. Change to needles one or two sizes larger for the remainder of the collar.

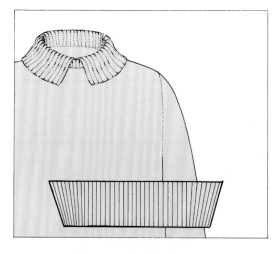

Polo Collar

Sometimes called a roll neck or a turtleneck, a polo collar is a straight tube or strip (depending on whether it is made on a set of four needles so avoiding a seam, or with a pair of needles) that fits on to a crew neckline. Extending a neckband that is worked from picked-up stitches gives the same effect.

The collar is knitted to twice the required length according to the depth of the neck that it must fit, then it is cast off very loosely or there is no chance of it fitting over a head. For wearing, the collar is doubled over to the right side.

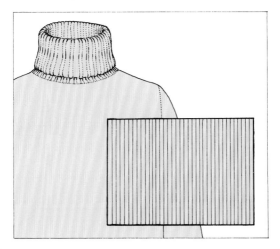

Cowl

Although they are constructed in the same way as polo collars, cowls are much wider and longer, so the finished effect is softer and draped rather than the close fit of a polo collar. To achieve this softer look cowls require the wider shaped base of a scoop neck. The cowl is usually very deep so that the fabric can be folded at least three times.

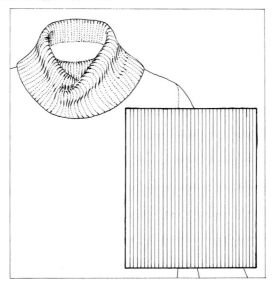

Shaped Shawl Collar

This collar is normally knitted separately, either vertically or horizontally, to fit a V neckline, and then the fabric is folded back on itself in a smooth, curved shape.

Vertically, knitting begins at the lower point of one front. To increase for the lapels one side is kept straight (always the outer edge for a better finish) while the other side is shaped to correspond with that of the V neckline. Once the fabric has reached its full width, the curves of the shoulder and back neck are negotiated with a series of shallow darts (see short-row knitting, pp.106–7) at each side. These extend the length of the outer – unshaped – edge, allowing it to turn back and sit neatly on the shoulders as the number of rows worked towards the edge increases. Reverse the shapings for the second side.

Following similar principles, a shawl collar can also be worked horizontally (as shown below).

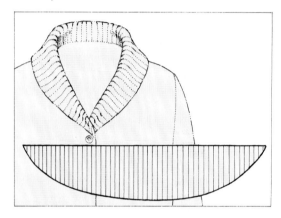

Basic Shawl Collar

Much simpler to work than a shaped shawl collar, a basic version consists of a straight strip that fits on to a square neckline to give a snug, semi-fitted effect. The cast-on edge must be the same length as the distance up one side of the front neck, across the back neck and down the second side of the front. The depth of the strip equals the distance across the base of the front neck.

In sewing up, the edges (row ends) are overlapped at the front and sewn down one on top of the other. For wearing, the extra fabric around the top and back neck is turned back on itself.

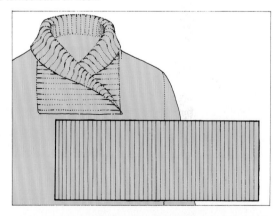

Sailor Collar

A sailor collar is a stylish trim for a square neckline that reflects its shape. The collar folds back on to the garment, away from the neck, at both the front and back. Unlike the other collars described here, a sailor collar is seldom worked in rib. Here it is a rectangle of stocking stitch with narrow garter stitch borders incorporated into the fabric at all edges, including those of the neck.

The neck shaping matches that of the main garment. Instead of casting off at the shoulders, the equivalent number of stitches cast off at the front neck are re-cast on for the back neck (joining the two shoulder sections) so that work continues in one piece for the back section of the collar. Sew the collar in place around the neck edge with a flat seam (see p.176), placing the right side of the collar to the wrong side of the neckline. Turn the collar through to the right side to hide the seam.

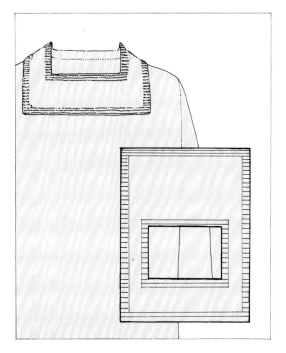

Tips

○ If there is a seam in a polo collar, reverse it half way so that the section of the outer edge shows on the right side of the garment. When the collar is folded over for wearing, it will be hidden.

○ Use a circular needle when making a cowl collar to avoid visible sections of seam once the fabric is folded.

Armholes and Sleeves

As fashion dictates styles, so knitting follows suit with changes in design that mark a garment as belonging to a particular era. Classic examples are the short, tight-waisted fitted cardigan of the 40/50s, the skinny rib polo neck of the 60s and the sloppy, loose, drop-shouldered sweater of the 70s.

The look of a garment can be varied according to the style of armhole, from subtle to dramatic features. The following examples describe the classic armhole shapes in knitwear and how to achieve them. Naturally sleeves must be matched to armholes, especially the section at the top where it fits on to the body.

Drop Shoulder

A drop shoulderline refers to a garment that has no shaping at the armholes, i.e. the side seams are absolutely straight up to the shoulders. Although the sides of the sleeve may be shaped in the usual way, the top should be straight to correspond with the body.

The drop-shouldered look has been adopted for loose and casual garments, especially since the rise in popularity of fancy or textured yarns; it is ideal for any garment where the main attraction is the yarn, textured stitches or patterned decoration, rather than the style of garment.

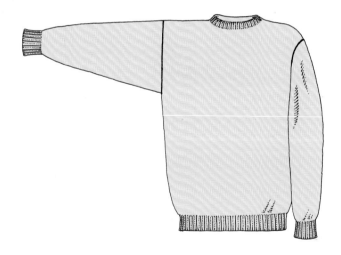

Although the basic styling could not be easier, care must be taken in assembling the garment. It is not sufficient to make up the body leaving a gap for sleeves to be sewn in later. In order that the sleeves are correctly placed the garment must be made up in a certain way. First, join the shoulder seams. Mark the underarm points on the back and front with a pin; patterns usually specify the depth, otherwise it is half the length across the top of the sleeve.

Mark the centre point on the sleeve top with a pin. Then, with right sides together, match the marked point to the shoulder seam on the opened-out back and front. Pin, then sew the sleeve in position between the underarm markers, avoiding any puckering in the fabric. Once the sleeve top is in place the side and sleeve seams can be joined in one continuous line.

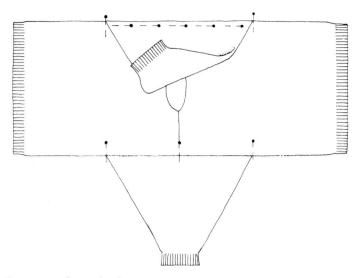

Square Armhole

A square armhole is similar to a drop shoulderline; again it is suitable for casual garments, particularly those worked in heavier yarns, because the shaping at the underarm minimizes the fabric at that point. It is also a half-way version of a set-in sleeve where the only shaping consists of a small group of cast-off stitches on a single row at the underarm. The remainder of the armhole up to the shoulder is worked straight. The sleeve used with a square armhole must be cast off with a straight edge across the top. Extra rows are worked straight at the top of the sleeve to fit along the cast-off underarm stitches.

When making up the garment, follow the same procedure as given for a drop shoulder – first setting in the sleeve top, matching the centre point to the shoulder seam before joining the sleeve and side seams. Sew the cast-off edge of the sleeve in position using a flat seam (see p.176) for the best result, then join the row ends at the top of the sleeve to the cast-off stitches at the underarm.

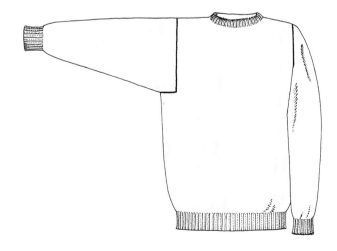

Set-in Sleeve

This classic armhole/sleeve shape suits a more fitted type of garment as the precise styling only looks good when the seam at the top of the sleeve falls on the exact shoulder line.

Back and front armhole shaping starts with a gradual curve at the underarm. First a small group of stitches are cast off on a single row, then stitches are decreased at the edges on every row (for approximately one-quarter of the armhole depth) until the edge is in line with the shoulder point. The remainder of the armhole is worked straight.

The top of the sleeve is a curved shape where the important fit is a combination of depth produced by rows and length around the perimeter from cast-off stitches, as well as the shaping involved earlier. Sleeve top shaping may vary according to the designer, but the process is basically the same. Initially cast-off stitches at either side correspond with those at the underarm, as do the following series of decreases. To round off towards the top of the curve, small sets of stitches are cast off at the beginning of every row leaving a short, straight section to be cast off for the top of the sleeve.

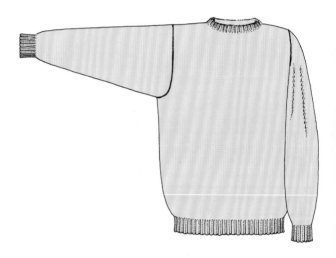

Setting In a Sleeve

To set in a sleeve requires some skill and practice as two different shapes must be fitted together. It differs from the other methods described so far in that the garment and sleeves must be made up separately so leaving a complete armhole for the sleeve to be fitted into. The finished sleeve should fit neatly into the armhole without any puckering.

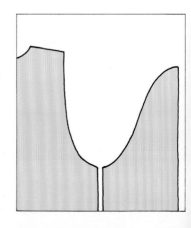

1 Join the shoulder and side seams on the garment in the usual way. Leave the garment wrong side out. Join the sleeve seam and turn the completed sleeve right side out. Fold the sleeve in half with the seam forming one side edge and mark the centre of the sleeve top with a pin.

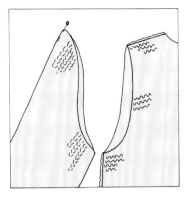

2 Position the sleeve inside the armhole with right sides together, matching underarm seams, and pin at sleeve top to the shoulder.

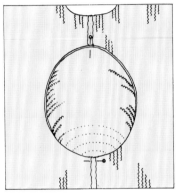

3 Pin the sleeve in position all round always working on the edge just inside the *sleeve* top. Match any shaping at underarms if possible and ease in any fullness (by placing pins at frequent intervals at right angles to the edge) on the sleeve top. Sew the sleeve in place with a back stitch seam following the line of pins inside the sleeve top edge.

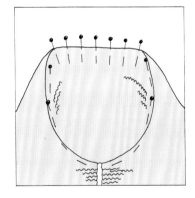

Saddle Sleeve

Often used for menswear, a saddle sleeve gives a more masculine square shoulder shape. A saddle yoke (as it is sometimes known) is a regularly shaped set-in sleeve top, but instead of casting off the last group of stitches you continue working on them. The extended strip fits along the width of the shoulder and, when the garment is made up, forms a small yoke. The sleeve fits into the same armhole as a set-in sleeve, only it must be shallower than normal to allow room for the yoke.

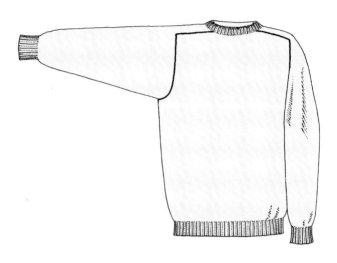

Raglan Sleeve

This popular sleeve is very versatile – a classic raglan that is fairly shallow is suitable for a more fitted garment while casual garments require a deeper, loose-fitting raglan. The raglan shape is a distinctive diagonal line produced by regular shaping at the side edges between the underarms (where there is usually a group of cast-off stitches) and the top of the sleeve. A raglan is peculiar in that the sleeve shaping matches that on the back and front of the garment so that they fit together exactly. A small group of stitches remaining at the end of the sleeve shaping forms part of the neck: they may be shaped to follow the curve of the neck.

Although the depth of a raglan can vary, the principle of shaping is always the same. Shallow, close-fitting raglans start at about the same underarm point as a set-in sleeve, but most are deeper and so require a shorter sleeve length.

Normal raglan shaping produces a rounded shoulder shape. For a jacket which needs more emphasis on the shoulders you can create a larger shoulder shape so that pads can be inserted – make an angle in the shaping by changing the frequency of decreasing from gradual (say, every fourth row) to steep (on every row, or alternate rows).

Tip

○ Emphasize raglan shaping so that it becomes a design feature. Paired decreases outline the edge – or you can insert a separate patterned or cabled band.

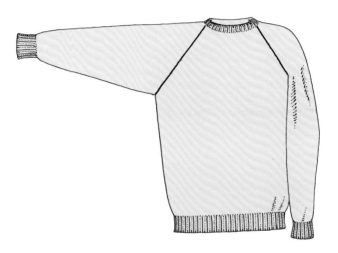

Sleeve shapes

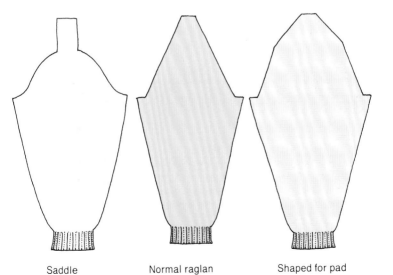

Saddle　　　　　Normal raglan　　　　Shaped for pad

Dolman Sleeve

This is a popular style for evening wear – the very wide sleeves have a draped effect. It is an impractical design for day wear as the bulk of fabric at the underarms does not fit easily under a jacket or coat.

When a dolman sleeve is knitted separately, it is shaped so that the top is extremely wide (about equal in length to the measurement from the wrist to underarm), then it is cast off in a straight line. The sleeve is set on to a straight (drop-shoulder) body edge starting at a point much lower than a normal sleeve – somewhere between the waist and underarm. To avoid great lengths of seaming it is quite common for a dolman sweater to be worked entirely in one piece – either from one lower edge, increasing out for the full width of the body and sleeves, working over the shoulders (incorporating the neck shaping), then decreasing down to the other edge. Or you can knit from cuff to cuff by starting at one cuff, making a sleeve, casting on the stitches for the side edge of the front and back, working across the body (incorporating the neck shaping), casting off the stitches for the other side edge, then working the second sleeve from the top down to the cuff. Both these methods involve increasing to a large number of stitches which can be worked more comfortably on a circular needle used to work in rows (see p.110).

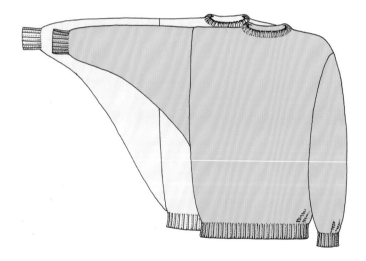

Batwing Sleeve

A batwing sleeve is a more dramatic version of a dolman. The top of the sleeve is extremely wide so that when it is joined to the body the sleeve seam forms a curved line from the waist to the cuff. Again, the sleeves can be knitted separately or the garment may be made in an entire piece.

Shoulder Pads

Many knitted garments, especially cardigans and jackets, benefit from the addition of shoulder pads – they change a mundane shape into one with style. Some garments are more suited to pads than others; these include loose garments with set-in sleeves, loose raglans, and garments such as dolmans that are knitted in one piece with no armhole seams.

Manufactured pads, made from moulded foam rubber, are ideal for heavy-weight yarns where extra shoulder definition is required. In certain circumstances bought pads may be preferable to knitted ones – raglan sleeves require the more rounded shape of an oval pad which is difficult to reproduce in knitting. The best pad for the majority of garments is triangular with one thicker edge. It should be knitted in garter stitch in the same yarn as the garment so that it does not show through on the right side of the work.

Making and Sewing in a Shoulder Pad

1 Using two strands of yarn, cast on two stitches. Increase one stitch at each end of every following alternate row until the pad is the required width (about 18cm/7in for an average adult garment). Work another 5cm (2in) without shaping, then cast off loosely.

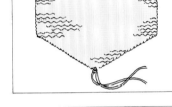

2 To thicken one edge, fold the straight section in half and slip stitch the cast-off edge in position along the last row of increasing.

3 Insert the pad into a hanging garment – not one that is inside out. The apex of the triangle should point to the neck. Hold it in position with pins inserted on the right side of the garment, matching up the centre of the pad with the shoulder seam and pinning the points of the triangle to the armhole seam. Turn the garment inside out to stitch the pad in place, only securing it at the points where it touches a seam; if it is sewn all round it will be very visible on the right side.

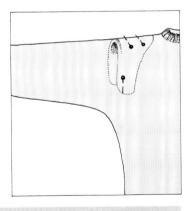

Tip

○ To make a firm, bulky shoulder pad, use the yarn double with the same size needles as the main fabric and work in garter stitch. To remove pads quickly and easily for washing, or when a garment has no seams, use a strip of Velcro fastening – sewing the hook side along the centre of the pad. If the yarn is fluffy the Velcro will cling directly to the fabric.

POCKETS

Pockets

When you put on a cardigan or jacket your hands instinctively reach for the pockets. Many garments feature pockets both for practical and decorative purposes. Although there are endless possibilities in style and design, types of pocket in everyday use fall into two main categories – those which are added after the completion of the garment (patch) and those which are an integral part of the design (horizontal and vertical). Details of working methods are included in pattern instructions, but with careful planning beforehand you can include pockets in garments where they are non-existent. Check first that the fabric is firm enough to support pockets. Then, to make them appear an integral part of the design rather than an afterthought, pockets should be in a complimentary style and stitch. Size and position can be checked by cutting out a paper template and pinning it to the garment: see that your hand fits in easily as it is easy to make pockets too small. Keep clear of any ribbed edges, hems, button bands or borders.

Most pockets require linings and a finishing border or edge usually referred to as the 'pocket top'. Linings should be knitted in the same yarn as the garment unless it is extremely thick or textured, where a finer, smoother yarn in a matching colour can be substituted. Whatever the pattern of the main fabric, linings should always be knitted in stocking stitch for a firm finish that will lie flat at the back of the work. Pocket tops follow the same rules as bands and borders (see pp.66–7); most are ribbed, but any firm stitch, such as garter or moss stitch, is suitable.

Patch Pockets

These are a piece of knitting applied to the right side of a completed garment: the actual garment forms the lining. Although square or rectangular pockets are the most popular, you can experiment with shapes and ideas. If you do not want a complicated shape, a pocket decorated with fancy stitches or embroidery is the perfect way of livening up a plain garment. The most difficult part of producing a patch pocket is sewing it neatly on to the background fabric.

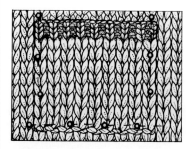

1 First pin the pocket in position on the background, aligning the edges so that they match up stitch for stitch and row for row.

2 To ensure that the edge will lie flat, use a slip stitch seam to sew the pockets in place.

Horizontal Pockets

A horizontal pocket is knitted into the garment as an integral part of the design. Working methods may vary, but in general a lining is made separately; at a later stage it replaces the stitches left for the opening at the top of the pocket.

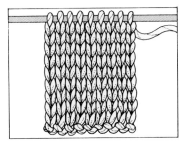

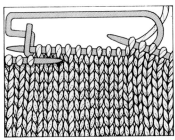

1 Before starting work on the main piece of fabric, cast on and work the pocket lining separately in stocking stitch, ending with a purl row. Patterns often quote a specific number of rows to ensure that the depth matches that of the main fabric row for row. Cut off the yarn and slip the stitches on to a spare needle.

2 Work on the main fabric as instructed in the pattern, generally allowing the same number of rows above the welt as there are in the lining. Continue until you reach the position of the opening on a right-side (knit) row: this row is often called the 'pocket row'. Slip the next group of stitches – corresponding in number to those of the lining – on to a holder.

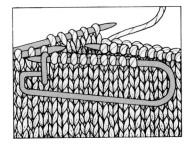

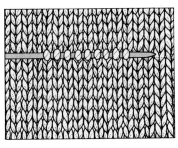

3 Instead of working on the stitches on the holder, work with those of the lining. Hold the lining stitches on the spare needle so that the right side of the lining is against the wrong side of the main fabric and knit across them. Continue knitting the stitches of the main fabric until you reach the end of the row.

4 After the main section of the garment is complete, the pocket stitches left on the holder are used to make a neatening border that is usually worked in rib. Using the same size needles as those used for the welt and with the right side of work facing, slip the stitches from the holder on to the left-hand needle. Join in the yarn and work in rib (you may be instructed to increase on the first row so that the border is not too tight) for about 3cm (1¼in). Cast off neatly in rib.

continued

5 Details of finishing off the pocket can be found in the 'making up' section of a pattern. First pin the lining in position on the wrong side, matching it to the correct number of rows and stitches to prevent the main fabric being pulled out of shape. Using a blunt-ended wool needle and matching yarn, slip stitch round the three sides of lining flap.

6 Complete the pocket on the right side of the work by sewing down the ends of the border: slip stitch them neatly in position using matching coloured yarn.

Vertical Pockets

Although similar to a horizontal pocket, a vertical pocket has an opening that goes down the rows rather than across a group of stitches. There is no need to work the lining separately; when you divide the work for the opening, you cast on extra stitches for the lining and knit it in one with the main fabric.

These instructions show how to insert a vertical pocket into the *left* front of a garment: for the right front, reverse the directions by reading knit for purl, right side for wrong side and vice versa.

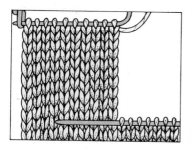

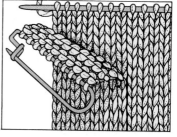

1 Work to the lower edge of the pocket on the main fabric. On a wrong-side row, purl to where the fabric is to be divided for the opening (about two-thirds of the way along). Turn and continue working on the first set of stitches only for one side of the opening until it is the required depth, ending with a wrong-side row. Cut off the yarn and leave these stitches on a holder.

2 Using the same ball of yarn, cast the pocket lining stitches on to the free needle. Take the needle with the cast-on stitches in your right hand; then, with the wrong side of the work facing, purl across the stitches on the left-hand needle that were left at the base of the opening. Continue in stocking stitch for the second side of the opening plus lining: work one row less than for the previous side, so ending with a right-side row.

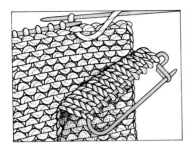

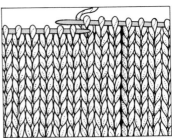

3 The lining is now complete. At the beginning of the next (purl) row, cast off the same number of stitches that you cast on previously for the pocket lining. Purl to the end of the row. Both sides of the opening are now complete.

4 Join the sections on the next row. Knit across the side just completed, then transfer the stitches from the holder on to the left-hand needle; knit across them. Beginning with a purl row, continue working the main fabric across all the stitches.

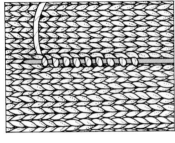

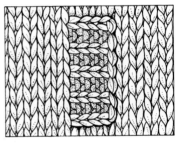

5 After finishing the main section, neaten the opening edge of the pocket with a border. Using the same size needles as those used for the welt (if the border is in rib) and with the right side of the work facing, pick up and knit the required number of stitches along the pocket edge.

6 Work about 3cm (1¼in) in rib, then cast off in rib. Complete the pocket lining on the wrong side of the work and sew down the ends of the pocket border on the right side as described for steps 5 and 6 of horizontal pockets (left).

Tips

○ Strengthen the weak points at either side of the pocket where it is joined to the main fabric by casting on two extra stitches for the lining. The extra stitches can be worked together – one at either side – with a stitch from the main fabric when the lining is knitted in.

○ Cast on using the thumb method (see p.43) for a pocket lining to produce an unobtrusive edge.

○ The lining of a vertical pocket always lies towards the centre front of a garment. If you adapt a cardigan pattern to include this type of pocket, make sure that it stays clear of the front edge.

Hems

Hems are used infrequently in knitting mainly because there are so many other finishing borders that are better suited to a knitted fabric. However, skirts, jackets or coats that are worked in a stitch that curls, such as stocking stitch, do require a hem as the weight of the double fabric benefits the hang of the hem. You can also use a hem as a casing for elastic (see p.98) or a drawstring. It is not always necessary for a hem to be at the lower edge of a garment; the same methods work equally well at any point on a garment where a tube effect is called for.

A hem must lie flat. Always work the section that is turned under in stocking stitch (the flattest fabric) regardless of the stitch used for the main fabric. The turned-under section should be worked at a tighter tension than the main fabric to make it lie neatly; if it is already firm, cast on (or decrease to) fewer stitches rather than change the needle size. There are two main types of horizontal hem – sewn or knitted-in. The other methods described here are interesting variations or alternatives.

Sewn Hem

Here the hem is sewn up after the garment has been completed.

1 For a hem at the lower edge, cast on using needles that are at least one size smaller than the main fabric. Beginning with a knit row, work an odd number of rows in stocking stitch until the hem is the required depth. Make a ridge on the right side of the fabric to create a sharp fold line by knitting (instead of purling) into the backs of the stitches in the next row. Change to the correct needle size and, starting with a knit or right-side row, complete the piece of knitting.

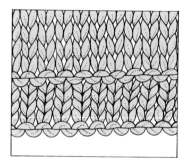

2 After the garment is complete, turn the hem to the wrong side at the fold line and pin it carefully in position keeping the cast-on edge straight in line with a row of knitting. Using a blunt-ended wool needle threaded with matching coloured yarn, sew the cast-on edge in position stitch for stitch. Take the needle through one cast-on loop and then through a stitch in the line of knitting directly above the hem. Work loosely or the fabric will pucker on the right side.

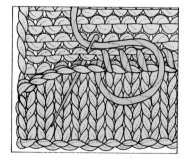

If the hem is at the end of a piece of knitting, you can follow the same instructions in reverse, sewing down the cast-off edge instead of the cast-on one. Alternatively for an elastic cast-off edge, an open edged hem is ideal (see p.96).

Tip

○ Hems require pressing, but this will not remedy any fault with knitting or making up. A hem that is lying badly must be re-sewn so that it is flat.

Knitted-in Hem

Whenever possible choose a knitted-in method of making a hem rather than a sewn one. It has a similar final appearance, but avoids the complications of sewing up the hem neatly. Before starting work check that you have to hand three needles one size larger than those used for the main fabric.

1 Work as given for step 1 of a sewn hem (left), knitting the top part of the hem on the main section until it is two rows less than the under section, ending with a right-side (knit) row. Using one size larger needle, purl the next row. Take another needle in the same size. With the right side of the work facing and the cast-on edge at the top, use the spare needle to pick up loops from the cast-on edge, working from left to right and slipping the needle from front to back through each loop. At the end count that there are the same number of stitches as were originally cast on.

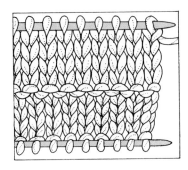

2 Fold the work in half, with the right side facing out, so that both needles are level and pointing in the same direction. Use the remaining needle in a larger size to knit both sets of stitches – taking one stitch from each needle together every time – so turning up the hem by knitting it into the fabric. The larger needles help to keep the tension correct; there is a tendency to work the hem row too tight which makes it prominent on the right side of the work. Change back to the correct size needles and continue with the main fabric.

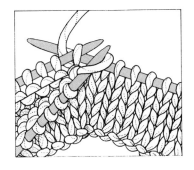

Open-edge Hem

Skirts are often knitted from the waistband down to the hem; coats and sweaters are sometimes worked in the same direction. If a hem is called for at the lower edge (i.e. the end of the knitted piece), do not cast off. Instead leave the stitches on the needle and cut off the yarn, so that a long length remains for sewing.

Thread the end of yarn into a blunt-ended sewing needle and, taking the stitches one by one from the knitting needle, hem them to the corresponding stitch several rows below – providing that there are the same number of stitches.

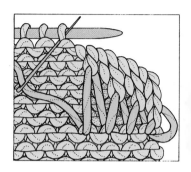

If there are less stitches in the hem edge than in the main piece miss a few stitches as required: where there are more stitches in the hem, sew two of them together to one of the stitches in the row of the main fabric where necessary.

Picot Hem

Picots are small loops of yarn with a twisted appearance that are used for decoration on edgings. A picot hem is an attractive variation of the hems described so far; it can either be knitted in or sewn up at a later stage. Instead of a fold line, a row of eyelet (small) holes (see lace knitting, p.154) marks the turn of the hem.

1 Cast on an odd number of stitches using needles that are at least one size smaller than the main fabric. Work in stocking stitch until the hem is the required depth, ending with a purl row. Work the eyelet-hole row as follows: K1, *yfwd (yarn forward, see p.154), K2 tog, rep from * to end. Change to the correct needle size. Starting with a purl or wrong-side row, either complete the hem or the piece of work depending on whether you are knitting-in or sewing up the hem.

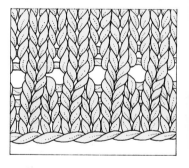

2 When the hem is turned up, the eyelets form a dainty, serrated or 'picot' edging that is particularly suitable for finer yarns or babywear.

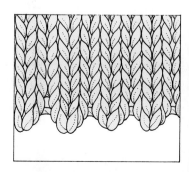

Mock Hem (for Ribbing)

This is really a form of invisible casting on that is applicable to ribbing. The bottom edge appears to have been neatly turned under, yet there is no double fabric and therefore no bulk. Use this technique where the ribbing is a main feature of a garment – an all-over rib pattern or a fitted sweater with a deep welt – rather than merely a finishing border.

Using yarn in a contrast colour, yet similar in thickness to the main yarn, cast on half the total number of stitches required. Cut off the contrast yarn and join in the main yarn. Continue as follows:

1st row K1, * yon (to make an extra st – see p.154), K1, rep from * to end.

2nd row K1, * yarn to front (ytf), sl 1 P-wise, yarn to back (ytb), K1, rep from * to end.

3rd row Sl 1 P-wise, * ytb, K1, ytf, sl 1 P-wise, rep from * to end.

4th–5th rows As 2nd and 3rd.

Now continue in ordinary K1, P1 rib as set for the required amount. After some distance you can unravel the contrast-coloured cast-on edge using the free needle point to gently ease the stitches apart.

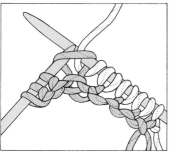

Working the first row in the main colour

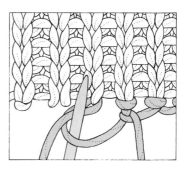

Unravelling the temporary cast-on edge

Tips

○ Keep a straight line when sewing by always working along the same row. Sew with a loose stitch that will give and not pull the main fabric.

○ Stitching must never show through on the right side of the work.

○ Do not use a hem with a lace or openwork pattern as it will show through on the right side.

○ An open-edged hem is a good way of sewing down a double neckband as the line of stitching is elastic.

Using Elastic

There are two, very different, types of elastic that are commonly used in knitting. One is very broad for grip in waistbands and the other is very fine for adding elasticity to areas where it is needed.

Elastic in Waistbands

Always use elastic that is specially made for waistbands – it is flat, ribbon-like and at least 2.5cm (1in) wide. Calculate the length of elastic you need by measuring it around your waist, stretching it slightly at the same time. Allow an extra 2.5cm (1in) for an overlap.

There are two methods of attaching the elastic – either enclosing it in a waistband or working a herringbone casing over it.

Threading Elastic through a Waistband Hem

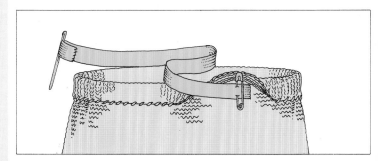

1 Make a hem (see p.90) that can be turned over to form a tube at the waist edge of the skirt. Join the side seams, then fold over the hem at the waist and slip stitch it in position, leaving about a 4cm (1½in) gap at one side seam.

2 After cutting the elastic, secure one end to the side seam with a safety pin. Insert the other end through the wide eye of a blunt-ended needle; double it back for a few centimetres and secure it with a few stitches so that it does not become unthreaded in the tube.

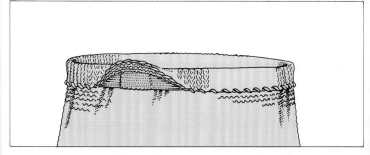

3 Thread the elastic through the casing. Join it into a circle by overlapping the ends and oversewing the elastic together

around the join. Make sure that the elastic is lying flat, then close up the opening.

Making a Herringbone Casing

This is a less bulky method than threading elastic through a hem as it does not involve two layers of knitted fabric. The elastic is held in place behind the waistband with a line of zigzag stitching.

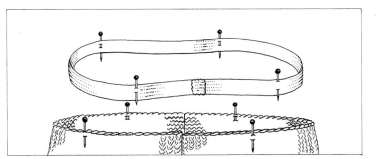

1 Cut the elastic to fit. Overlap the ends to make a circle and secure by oversewing them. Mark the circle into four equal sections with pins.

2 Join the skirt seams. Divide the upper edge into quarters, marking the four points with pins. On the wrong side of the waistband, pin the elastic in position matching the quarter-section pins on the elastic and skirt. (Naturally, the circle of elastic is much tighter than the top of the skirt so it will pull it in considerably.)

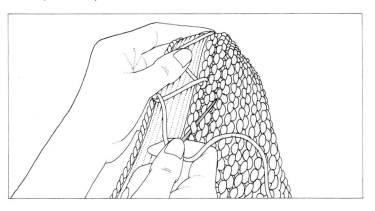

3 Thread a blunt-ended wool needle with matching-coloured yarn and work a herringbone stitch over the elastic as shown. You will need to stretch the elastic as you are sewing by holding a section of waistband and the elastic taut over the fingers of your left hand as you are working.

Shirring/Knitting-in Elastic

Both these types of elastic thread are added to yarns with little or no elasticity – such as cotton and linen – during knitting. They are a preventative measure to keep areas that need grip (especially ribbed welts, cuffs and neckbands) in shape. As a rescue measure, elastic can give life back to the same ribbed areas that have stretched during wash and wear, or that have been worked too loosely in the first place.

Shirring elastic

This is the original thin elastic thread (available on a reel) that was widely used before the advent of knitting-in elastic. It should be possible to obtain either a transparent shirring elastic or one in a colour that matches the yarn, in which case it can be knitted together with the yarn.

If there is any doubt about the colour match, the elastic can still be worked in with the ribbing, but it must be stranded across the back of the work. On right-side rows the elastic is woven behind every knit stitch and in front of purl stitches on wrong-side rows (see pp.140–2 for more details on stranding and weaving techniques).

For out-of-shape ribbing, sew in shirring elastic with running stitches on alternate rows on the wrong side of the work. Remember to keep an even tension – one that resembles the natural tension of the yarn is best so that there is no obvious 'gathering' of the fabric.

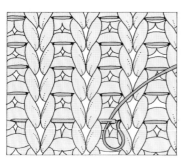

Stranding shirring elastic across the back of the work

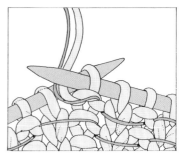

Sewing in shirring elastic

Knitting-in elastic

A more up-to-date equivalent of shirring elastic, the knitting-in variety is a very fine thread with incredible stretch. Usually available in its natural state which is shiny and see-through, this form of elastic is invisible when used with the yarn. As it blends so well with most colours, knitting-in elastic is applied exactly as its name implies – one ball of yarn and one reel of elastic are worked together where necessary.

Tips

○ Use knitting-in elastic to add strength to stress points on garments knitted in delicate fibres, such as mohair or silk.

○ Before cutting elastic for a waistband, pin and wear it for a while to check for comfort.

Pleats and Tucks

The technique of making pleats and tucks involves folding layers of knitted fabric back upon itself. A pleat is a vertical line of folded fabric. While pleats are an obvious style feature for a skirt, they can also be used as an inset detail on the body of a blouse or jacket. For an inset, extra stitches for the folds must be cast on at intervals across the row where the pleats start.

A tuck is really a horizontal pleat. Tucks are useful purely for decoration or for highlighting features on otherwise plain garments – the hem of a dress or skirt, the yoke of a blouse or jacket or where the sleeves of a horizontally knitted dolman sweater meet the body.

Neither pleats nor tucks are suitable for heavy yarns because of the bulk of the fabric. Basic pleats and tucks must be worked in a smooth flat fabric such as stocking stitch. Although knitted pleats can never equal the knife-sharpness of cloth ones, you can use technical tricks to achieve effective results. Alternatively let the knitted fabric work to your advantage: choose the right stitch and you can produce mock pleats with very little effort.

Knife Pleats

It is quite easy to adapt a skirt pattern, or to make up your own design, to include inverted pleats. The width of the cast-on hem must be three times the waist measurement. Ensure that the number of stitches is divisible by 12 plus eight extra stitches.

The main fabric is knitted straight up from the hem with marker stitches to denote folds – a purl stitch for the under fold line and a slip stitch for the upper one. Pleats are knitted into position on the last row: for this you will need two extra needles with points at both ends.

Variations of knife pleats include *box pleats* where one knife pleat pointing to the right and one pointing to the left are facing away from each other; also *inverted pleats* where right and left pointing knife pleats are facing each other. *Soft pleats* can be formed in the same way as knife pleats, but without the fold lines, the pleats are simply closed at the top edge. Do not form any sharp creases when pressing a softly pleated fabric.

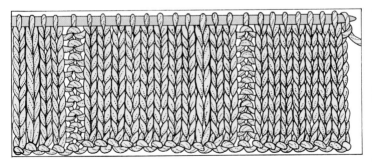

1 Cast on a multiple of 12 plus 8 extra stitches and work as follows:
1st row (RS) * K8, P1, K2, sl 1 P-wise, rep from * to last 8 sts, K8.

2nd row * P11, K1, rep from * to last 8 sts, P8. Repeat these two rows for the required length, ending with a wrong-side row. *continued*

2 Use the two double-pointed needles to knit-in the pleats on the last row. **Last row** (RS) K4, * sl next 4 sts on to first extra needle, sl next 4 sts on to second extra needle, then place first extra needle behind second one and hold both needles behind left-hand needle, (K tog one st from each of 3 needles) 4 times, rep from * to last 4 sts, K4. After drawing a loop through the three stitches being worked together, carefully drop the stitches from each of the needles individually.

3 The last row automatically pleats the fabric. Keep the edge of the pleats in place by running a tacking thread along them, then block and press the fabric (see pp.173–4). Tack the pleats in position each time the garment is washed or cleaned.

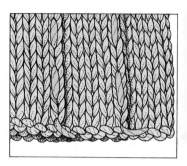

Mock Pleats

These give the appearance of a pleated fabric without any folding or layering. A garter or purl stitch fabric is broken into sections with a single knit stitch (rather like a wide rib) – a line of which resembles a fold.

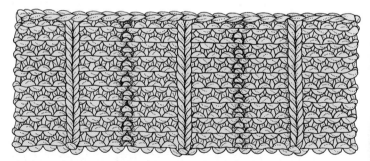

1 Cast on a number of stitches that is divisible by 8 and work as follows: **1st row** (RS) * K7, P1, rep from * to end. **2nd row** K4, * P1, K7, rep from * to last 4 sts, P1, K3. Repeat these two rows for the required length, then cast off in pattern. The fabric automatically gathers up vertically into mock pleats. The alternating chain stitch on either side of the work gives the fabric a ribbed effect as well as acting as a fold line.

2 Shaping to avoid bulk around the hips is easy to achieve with mock pleats. Simply decrease two stitches in each section by working two stitches together at either side of the single 'chain' stitch on the side of the work facing you.

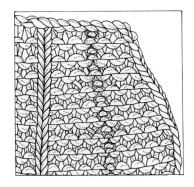

Making a Tuck

The method of working a tuck is similar to that of a hem – it is knitted into the body of a fabric rather than being worked at the beginning or end.

The concertina effect of tucks is perfect for coloured stripes – either in subtle shades of one colour or boldly bright with a different colour for each tuck.

1 Work in stocking stitch to the position of the tuck, ending with a purl row. Tie a marker loop of different-coloured yarn to the stitch at each end of the last row. (Alternatively, use a plastic marker.) Now you must work a number of rows that will be folded back on themselves to form the tuck. Depending on the depth required for one side, work an odd number of rows, ending with a knit row. Make a fold line so that the tuck will turn neatly by knitting all the stitches in the next row through the back of the loops to form a ridge on the right side of the fabric. Beginning with a knit row, work the second side of the tuck; it will have one less row than the first, so ending with a purl row.

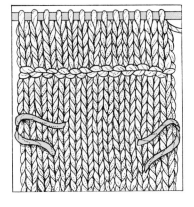

2 With the wrong side of the work facing and using a needle one or two sizes smaller than those used for the main fabric, start at the right-hand edge of the marked row and pick up the correct number of stitches along it, inserting the needle from right to left under the top loop of each stitch. Check that the points of both needles – that holding the stitches and the spare one – are facing in the same direction.

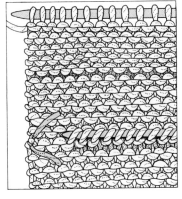

continued

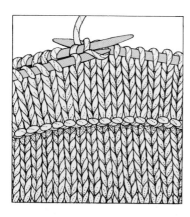

3 Knit the tuck into position. With the spare needle behind the one holding the stitches, work to the end of the row knitting two stitches together – one from each of the needles – every time.

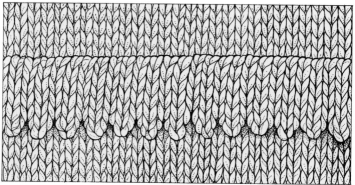

4 A picot edging makes a dainty alternative to a fold line. It uses the same techniques as a picot hem (see p.96). After working the first side of the tuck, ending with a knit row, make a line of eyelet holes on the next row (knit two stitches together, then bring the yarn forward to make a stitch, all along the row). Complete the tuck as described above. When it is folded along the line of eyelet holes, a picot edge is formed.

Tips

○ As pleats are formed with three thicknesses of fabric, avoid using them where they would be too bulky (i.e. around the hips). Instead, work a flat hip yoke and start the pleats lower down.

○ If you are adding pleats or tucks to a design remember to allow more yarn than stated in the pattern.

○ When making a skirt, use a yarn that will retain its shape without dropping: pure wool crepe is ideal for this purpose.

○ A pleated skirt will have a large number of stitches. Use a circular needle and work in the round to make it in one piece, or work backwards and forwards in rows if it is in two sections.

Short-row Knitting

This is a method of shaping where the work is turned before the entire row has been completed, so making one side of the fabric longer than the other – hence its alternative name of 'turning rows'. Always remember to measure the work along the shorter edge to obtain an accurate length.

Shaping work in this way produces a flat triangular wedge of fabric that is ideal for making darts, curves, frills and flares. However, only use these shapings when working in a plain stitch (such as stocking stitch) in a single colour: they are not advisable for stitch or colour patterns.

Use darts on skirts or trousers where the centre back must be deeper than the side seams or at the centre back of a collar which must be deeper than the sides so that it folds back and sits properly.

Short-row knitting is a useful flat method of making circular shapes for cushions, mats or decorative purposes. The only drawback is that the circular shape does require a seam. The circle usually comprises between six and 16 twirling, wedge-shaped sections – or darts – (in this case each one could be knitted in a different colour). The basic principle for forming a circle is the same as that given for curves (see p.108) except that there are no rows between the darts at the inner edge (i.e. the centre of the circle). Stitch the two identical shapes together around the outer edges to form the casing for a soft ball.

How to Avoid Holes

If you just turn the work in the middle of a row, there will be a noticeable hole at the turning point. Follow the simple rules shown here to prevent an unsightly hole appearing (assuming that the fabric is in stocking stitch).

1 On a right-side row, knit to the turning point. Bring the yarn forward to the front of the work and slip the next stitch knitwise. Take the yarn to the back again and return the slipped stitch to the left-hand needle. Turn the work and purl to the end of the row. *continued*

2 Continue in this way, working rows that are gradually shorter than the previous one, until the required depth has been reached, ending with a purl row. The final row is worked across all the stitches, closing the holes formed by turning.

3 To work the last row, knit to the first stitch that has a loop of yarn across the front of it and knit this stitch. Use the left-hand needle point to pick up the loop lying across the front of the last stitch and knit it together with the next stitch on the left-hand needle. Continue in this way to the end of the row.

4 The method described here is a useful way of shaping a shoulder to avoid the 'stepped' effect of groups of cast-off stitches. Instead of casting off stitches at the beginning of alternate rows, work turning rows. On the last row cast off all the stitches, closing the holes as shown in step 3, to make a smooth slope.

Making a Horizontal Dart

A dart is a triangular wedge of fabric created by short-row knitting that lengthens one edge of the fabric. The knitted method is superior to a sewn dart where layers of fabric are folded and stitched; here the fabric is actually shaped as you are working.

Placing darts is quite easy; they can be positioned exactly where the shaping is required. The most easily recognizable are bust darts – shaped from the centre of a row outwards, but collars can be shaped to the right or left (depending on the neckline) by leaving unworked stitches at the right or left edge, or increasing the width so that the centre back is deeper than the sides.

The mechanics of making a horizontal dart are basically the same as given for 'avoiding holes' (see p.105). To work out how many stitches and rows are required, calculate how deep the dart needs to be and translate this measurement into a number of rows according to the tension. Halve the number of rows as turning occurs only on alternate ones. Now decide how many stitches there are in the length of the dart. Divide by the number of rows to give the number of stitches in each turning group: if there are extra stitches distribute them among the groups (it does not matter if they vary slightly in number).

Following the steps given for 'avoiding holes', work across all the stitches in the dart (i.e. the entire length) to the first turning point. After that the turning rows become progressively shorter – reducing by one group of stitches each time – until the final group has been worked. To continue with the main fabric, work across all the stitches in the row closing the holes as shown.

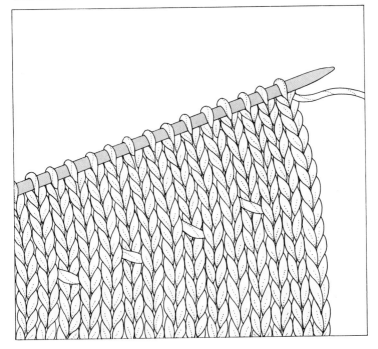

Tips

○ Darts – where shaping is worked within the fabric – are only suitable for stocking stitch worked in one colour. Stitch or colour patterns would be badly interrupted by the shaping.

○ Where two darts are symmetrical such as those at the bust of a blouse, turning takes place at the right-hand edge on knit rows and at the left-hand edge on purl rows.

Making a Mitre

Turning rows in the form of a double horizontal dart make a very neat mitred corner. Use this method of turning a corner for a border that is being worked in one direction rather than where the horizontal and vertical edges are at right angles (see p.77 for details of mitring a corner on a square neckline).

The general formula for turning a corner consists of leaving one stitch unworked, then one more stitch on each alternate row for the entire width of stitches, then repeating the reverse procedure, working one more stitch every time. The instructions given here make no attempt to close the holes left by turning; instead a diagonal line of them makes an attractive feature of the turn.

To make the border shown here, work up to the point of the corner, ending at the outside edge. **Next row** K to last st, turn. **Next row** K to end. **Next row** K to last 2 sts, turn. Continue in this way, leaving one more stitch unworked on every alternate row until one stitch remains. **Next row** K2, turn. **Next row** K to end. **Next row** K3, turn. Now work as set, including one more stitch on alternate rows until you are again working across all the stitches, then continue straight without shaping until the inner edge is the required length.

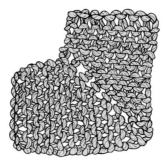

Making a Curve

To shape a curved edge on a piece of knitting use a series of darts to form a smooth curve instead of various shapings at the side edges (increases, decreases, cast-on/off groups) which leave a ragged edge. This type of shaping, especially when it is continued at regular intervals, is used for collars, circular yokes, skirts and berets.

You can assess the degree of curve required by calculating the number of rows along the inner edge of the curve and the extra number to go round the longer, outer edge. Say there are 40 extra rows at the outer edge, then you could work four darts of ten rows deep or five darts of eight rows. In general, working more, shallower darts helps to keep the curve smooth. Worked along the entire length of the row, the darts are inserted at regular spacing along the inner edge.

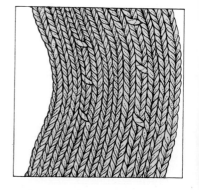

Circular Knitting

In the past all knitting used to be produced 'in the round' (another term for circular knitting), which meant that garments had virtually no seams. As knitting has become more of a leisure activity, rather than an industry, and garments are required to have more style in terms of shaping, then flat knitting – working in rows – has grown in popularity.

These days circular knitting is mainly confined to small items or areas – gloves, socks, hats, neckbands and armbands – which is a shame as many knitters detest assembling a garment, something that is hardly ever necessary with one that is knitted in the round.

Garments that are still constructed along traditional lines – that is knitted in the round up to the yoke or shoulders and with sleeves worked likewise down from the armholes – are Guernsey sweaters. Further details of knitting these garments are given on pp.112–4.

Circular knitting has many advantages: speed – the work is never turned; helps even tension – the right side always faces you, which means that stocking stitch is formed by knitting every row, so there is no purl row (often, inadvertently, worked at a tighter tension); texture or colour patterns – with the right side facing, it is easy to keep track of where you are in the pattern; Fair Isle patterns – the colours not in use are always at the back of the work and in the correct position when they are needed.

Adapting a Pattern

There are still many instances where a knitter who prefers working in the round can adapt instructions for a garment worked on two needles. Look at the instructions before starting work and sort out how you are going to transcribe them. For armholes or other openings it is best to divide the work and continue in flat knitting, shaping as required.

Calculate the number of cast-on stitches by adding the front and back stitches together and subtracting any extra edge stitches that may have been added to the original. For garments with a pattern repeated across the row, there must be a complete number of repeats. Either subtract the odd edge stitch or see if another repeat will fit in after the front and back edge stitches have been combined, adding extra stitches if necessary. Keep patterns correct by reversing all wrong-side rows, reading them from the end and working knit for purl and purl for knit.

Tips

○ If you are using scraps of yarn and making up a pattern or design as you go along, working in the round will ensure that the design is the same back and front. For two sleeves to match, work at the same time on a *pair* of needles.

○ The nylon wire joining the two tips of a circular needle is usually twisted. To straighten it, dip it in hot water, then pull it taut between thumb and forefinger.

CIRCULAR KNITTING

Using a Circular Needle

For circular knitting you require either a circular needle or a set of needles. In general, a circular needle is used where there is a large number of stitches (for a big circle such as a sweater) and a set of needles for smaller items or numbers of stitches.

Circular needles are available in varying lengths; it is important to choose the correct one for your work. If the length is not stipulated in the pattern, pick a needle according to the *minimum* number of stitches that you will be using. The needle should be smaller than the circle you are making as stretching stitches affects the tension. However, if the number of stitches varies dramatically with the shaping, you may have to use different lengths of needle to prevent the stretching, or overcrowding, of stitches.

1 Cast on carefully, allowing the stitches to overflow from the rigid needle section onto the nylon wire. When the total number of stitches has been cast on they should reach comfortably from the right-hand needle point to the left-hand one. Tie a marker loop of contrast-coloured yarn to the left-hand needle point.

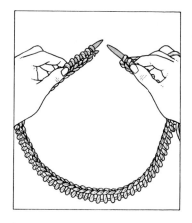

2 Before starting to knit, check that the cast-on stitches are not twisted. Slip the marker loop onto the right-hand needle, then knit the first stitch on the left-hand needle; pull the yarn across quite tightly to avoid making a loose stitch at this join. Continue working the row, gradually moving the stitches from the wire into the knitting position on the left-hand needle. You have come to the end of the first round when you reach the marker loop on the left-hand needle; slip the marker on to the right-hand needle before beginning the second, or subsequent, rounds. By knitting every stitch in every round a tubular stocking stitch fabric soon begins to take shape.

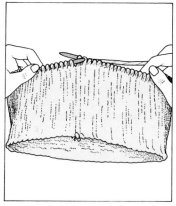

Using a Set of Needles

Three of the four needles in a set hold the stitches in a triangular shape; the fourth needle is held in the right hand and is used to knit the stitches. When all the stitches from one needle have been knitted, that needle becomes the working needle. At first you may find it quite difficult to work in this way as the needles are awkward to manage, but it becomes easier with practice.

1 Cast the total number of stitches required on to one of the four needles (or any needle that is the correct size and long enough). Divide the stitches equally between three needles that represent the left-hand needle in flat knitting and tie a marker loop of contrast-coloured yarn to the left-hand end of the stitches to denote the beginning of new rounds.

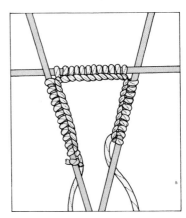

2 Arrange the stitches in a triangle – they must not be twisted – ready to begin knitting. Take the fourth – or right-hand needle and slip the marker loop on to it. To join the triangle, insert the fourth needle into the first stitch on the third needle and knit it in the usual way. Always pull the yarn across tightly from the previous stitch when changing needles to avoid loose stitches. Continue knitting in a clockwise direction, working the stitches on the third needle until it becomes free. Use this free needle to knit the stitches on the second needle and, in turn, use the free second needle to work the stitches on the first needle to complete one round.

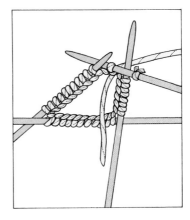

Constructing a Guernsey Sweater

Guernseys, or 'ganseys' as they are sometimes known, were typical, practical working sweaters produced in fishing communities around the British Isles from the end of the eighteenth century until the decline of fishing as a major industry and the arrival of mass-produced industrial knitwear. Although no longer traditionally produced, guernseys are popular as casual or sportswear.

The trademarks of a guernsey are easy to distinguish – first by the distinctive stitch patterns and secondly their method of construction. There is a number of different ways of producing a guernsey, but the principle is the same for all of them – for added strength the body is knitted in rounds on a circular needle, while the sleeves are worked downwards in rounds on a set of four needles using stitches picked up from around the armholes. The sweater shown here is divided at the armholes so that the top sections of the back and front are completed separately using rows of flat knitting. Other designs may be completely tubular with the armhole divisions marked by long horizontal strands of yarn made by winding the yarn a number of times round the needle on one round and dropping the extra loops on the next. When the body is complete the strands are cut down the centre to open the armhole, then each strand is darned in on the wrong side of the work.

○ Traditional guernsey worn by fishermen circa 1909.

Another important characteristic feature of a guernsey is the underarm gusset, which is a diamond-shaped piece of knitting set into the side seam of a garment before the armhole division and eventually carried on into the top of the sleeve seam. As most of the original fishermen's garments were made to be close-fitting and in thick yarn for extra warmth, a gusset was essential as it allowed for ease of movement.

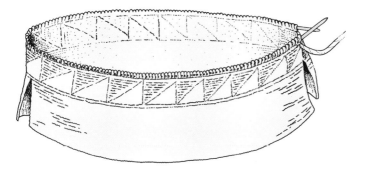

1 The lower edge of the body often consists of separate back and front sections with side slits to give extra movement. The flaps are knitted in a firm fabric (such as garter stitch) on a pair of needles and joined into a tubular fabric (often with a narrow, ribbed trim) on a circular needle.

2 The body is worked in rounds on the circular needle with a single line of vertical purl stitches at either side above the slits denoting the side 'seams'. Towards the top of the side 'seams' the first, triangular sections of gusset are shaped by increasing at either side of the marked 'seam' line on alternate rows. After the gussets are completed, the work is divided so that the front and back can be finished separately by working in rows with a pair of needles. The gusset stitches are held on a length of thread.

continued

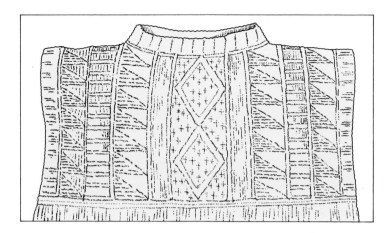

3 To complete the back and front armholes, continue without shaping to the shoulders. Cast off the shoulder stitches and continue in rib on the centre stitches for a small, stand-up neckband. Often guernsey-style stitch patterns adorn the yoke from the underarm upwards.

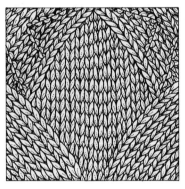

4 To work the sleeves, first join the shoulder seams. Using a set of needles pick up the sleeve stitches from around the armholes including the gusset. As the sleeve progresses downwards the gusset stitches are gradually decreased until it is a diamond shape (triangular in profile) when the garment is folded. The remaining gusset stitch forms the sleeve 'seam' stitch: sleeve shaping occurs at either side of the 'seam' stitch at regular intervals to narrow the sleeve towards the cuff. Work a ribbed cuff at the end of the sleeve before casting off.

Tips

○ It is easy to lose track of the beginning of a new round in circular knitting. Use a marker loop of contrast-coloured yarn to denote a new round and slip it from one needle to the other each time.

○ Avoid loose stitches when changing needles. Always start a new needle so that it is in position on top of the old one; pull the first stitch tight.

○ If a twisted cast-on edge is a problem, try casting on with two needles in the usual way. Work one row, then divide the stitches between three double-pointed needles and continue the rounds.

Aran Knitting

The most popular form of classic knitting is historically and romantically linked to the Aran Islands, which lie off the west coast of Ireland. Supposedly fishermen's work-wear, there is little factual proof that the garments we know as Aran sweaters were even actually produced on the islands – if they were, it was not in any great numbers and in comparatively recent times. Certainly the islanders produced the handspun, creamy, undyed wool – called 'bainin' – that is traditional for Aran sweaters. It is ideal for fishermen or seamen as the lanolin content makes it water repellent. These days, although Aran-type yarn is widely available, the vast and diverse range of patterns can be produced in other types of yarn, providing scope for anything from rugged sportswear to delicate evening wear.

The most distinctive feature of Arans today are the heavily embossed fabrics which, unlike other fishermen's sweaters or 'guernseys', have always been worked in flat sections rather than on circular needles. Again, the exact influences on the designs are unclear. There are obvious links with ancient Celtic culture in the Aran islands, but the garments that we recognize today as characteristically Aran are probably based upon Central European styles of knitting that were popular earlier this century.

It is likely that the growth of the Aran knitting industry is linked with the potato famines that ravaged Ireland in the late 19th century. Cottage industries were encouraged by the government, so providing an income to alleviate the appalling poverty.

The endless elements used in Aran stitch patterns are said – in common with other forms of folk knitting – to have been used by the islanders to describe their heritage. Plants, animals, the daily patterns of working life all assume a special significance. Cables are obviously 'ropes', while other sections of the design depict some everyday object or event. The following are a few 'translations' of popular Aran patterns: *Aran moss stitch* – the raised texture represents the stony island soil; *diamond pattern* – echoes the shape of the fishing net mesh (they can mean wealth or small, stony fields when filled in with moss stitch); *honeycomb pattern* – represents hard work and rewards (as related to bees producing honey); *bobbles* – echo rocks and boulders; *zig-zag lines* – indicate cliff paths or lightning.

Traditional Aran garment styles are classical with the emphasis on the surface patterning. Individual knitters use clever mixtures of familiar patterns; often a garment has a wide central panel framed by cables and side sections featuring a textured background.

Whatever the fact or fiction surrounding it, Aran, as a style of knitting, has been popular for more than 50 years. The rich source of patterns affords endless scope for designers, not only for Aran garments, but the techniques provide inspiration for many other types of design.

○ This modern Aran cardigan incorporates traditional Aran design features.

Cables

Aran knitting is immediately recognizable by its use of cable in all forms – as a decorative panel, in conjunction with other stitches or as an all-over fabric. Usually cables are worked as knit stitches shown in sharp relief against the purl background. The even number of stitches in a cable are divided into two equal sets when crossing occurs on the right side of the work.

Only two techniques are involved in making a cable – either crossing the stitches to the right (back) or to the left (front). To cross the stitches one set is held on a spare (cable) needle until it is transferred to another position a few stitches further on. Variations of cable are effected by altering either the width in stitches, or the number of rows between crossing or the sequence of right or left crossings or a combination of these.

Cables can dramatically affect the width of a fabric, sometimes drawing it in by as much as a third. To avoid a 'fluted' welt, fewer stitches are cast on and an increase row is worked at the top of the welt. Increases should be positioned where they are required – at the base of any cables.

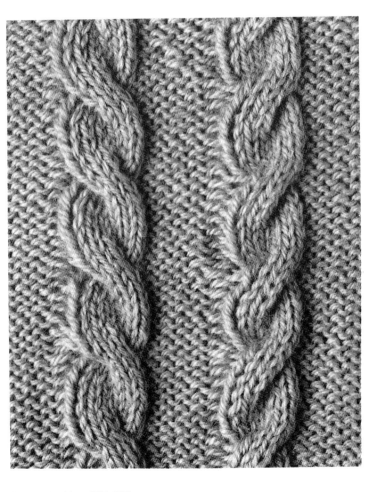

Standard cable – C6B, C6F

Cable variations – C8B

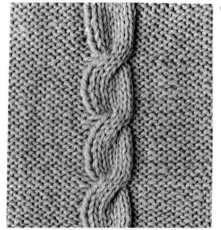

Greater distance between twists

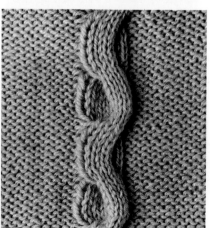

Alternating twists

How to Make a Cable

Crossing to the right – cable 6 back (C6B)

1 Work to the position of the cable column (i.e. here it is six knitted stitches against a purl background). Slip the next three stitches on to a cable needle and leave it at the *back* of the work. Continue to knit the remaining three stitches in the column, pulling the yarn tightly across.

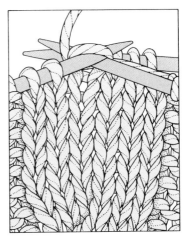

2 Push the stitches on the cable needle to the right-hand end, close to the right-hand needle, so that they can be knitted. (The cable needle is finished with for the time being.) Continue to work to the position of the next cable or the end of the row. On subsequent rows the cable column is worked in stocking stitch without any shaping until the next 'cable' row is reached.

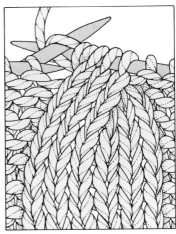

Crossing to the left – cable 6 front (C6F)

Work as given for step 1 of twisting a cable to the right, but leave the stitches on the cable needle at the *front* of the work. Complete as given for step 2.

Cable Variations

Using the basic techniques it is possible to create many cable patterns. The following designs show a variety of cables as single panels.

Alternating cable

(Worked over 9 sts)
1st row (RS) K9.
2nd row P9.
3rd row Sl next 3 sts on to cable needle and leave at back of work, K3, then K the 3 sts from cable needle (called C6B), K3.
4th row P9.
5th–6th rows As 1st and 2nd.
7th row K3, sl next 3 sts on to cable needle and leave at front of work, K3, then K the 3 sts from cable needle (called C6F).
8th row P9.
These 8 rows are repeated to form patt.

Horseshoe cable

(Worked over 12 sts)
1st row (RS) K12.
2nd row P12.
3rd–4th rows As 1st and 2nd.
5th row Sl next 3 sts on to cable needle and leave at back of work, K3, then K the 3 sts from cable needle (CB6), sl next 3 sts on to cable needle and leave at front of work, K3, then K the 3 sts from cable needle (CF6).
6th row P12.
7th–8th rows As 1st and 2nd.
These 8 rows are repeated to form patt.

Plaited cable

(Worked over 18 sts)
1st row (RS) K18.
2nd row P18.
3rd row (Sl next 3 sts on to cable needle and leave at back of work, K3, then K the 3 sts from cable needle) 3 times.
4th row As 2nd.
5th–6th rows As 1st and 2nd.
7th row K3, (sl next 3 sts on to cable needle and leave at front of work, K3, then K the 3 sts from cable needle) twice, K3.
8th row As 2nd.
These 8 rows are repeated to form patt.

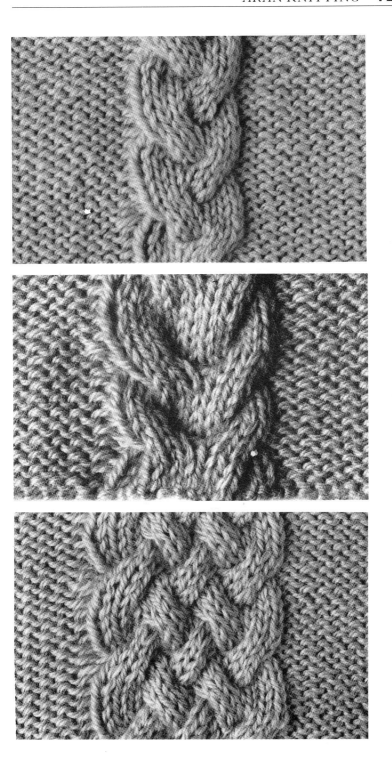

Travelling Stitches

These stitches twist and intertwine to form miniature cables, diamond shapes and zig-zag patterns. They can be used as a substitute for cables or in conjunction with them in Aran designs, either in panels or as an all-over pattern.

The technique of twisting stitches is worked over a small number of stitches – two or three is usual. Quite often a single knit stitch moves across a background in a continuous line with twists occurring on every row rather than at intervals as with cables. One method of twisting stitches – either to the right or left – requires a cable needle while an alternative way twists the stitches on the working needle so producing a mock cable.

Twisting stitches to the right – (Tw2R)

1 Miss the first stitch on the left-hand needle and knit into the second one without dropping it from the needle (the first, unworked, stitch is blocking the way).

2 Now knit the first stitch as normal and allow the original loops of both stitches to fall from the left-hand needle.

3 For an interesting mock cable alternative to K2, P2 rib, work as follows: cast on a multiple of 4 sts + 2 sts. **1st row** (RS) P2, * Tw2R, P2, rep from * to end. **2nd row** K2, * P2, K2, rep from * to end. Rep these 2 rows to form patt.

Twisting stitches to the left – (Tw2L)

Work as given for twisting stitches to the right, but in step 1 knit into the back of the second stitch on the left-hand needle.

Travelling Stitch Patterns

Fabrics involving travelling or crossed stitches are popular not only in Aran knitting, but also as textured fabrics (see Net Lattice and Diamond Lattice, pp.124–5). The Diamond Panel illustrates the technique of crossing stitches using a cable needle as opposed to an ordinary needle.

Diamond panel

(Worked over 14 sts)

1st row (RS) P5, K4, P5.

2nd and foll alt rows K all sts that were purled in previous row and P all sts that were knitted.

3rd row P5, sl next 2 sts on to cable needle and leave at front of work, K2, then K the 2 sts from cable needle (called C4F), P5.

5th row P4, sl next st on to cable needle and leave at back of work, K2, then K1 from cable needle (called Cr2R), sl next 2 sts on to cable needle and leave at front of work, P1, then K2 from cable needle (called Cr2L), P4.

7th row P3, Cr2R, P1, K1, Cr2L, P3.

9th row P2, Cr2R, (P1, K1) twice, Cr2L, P2.

11th row P1, Cr2R, (P1, K1) 3 times, Cr2L, P1.

13th row P1, Cr2L, (K1, P1) 3 times, Cr2R, P1 from cable needle instead of K1, P1.

15th row P2, Cr2L, (K1, P1) twice, Cr2R as 13th row, P2.

17th row P3, Cr2L, K1, P1, Cr2R as 13th row, P3.

19th row P4, Cr2L, Cr2R as 13th row, P4.

20th row As 2nd.

The 3rd–20th rows are repeated to form patt.

Net Lattice
(Worked over 16 sts plus 2 extra)
1st and every foll alt row (WS) P to end.
2nd row K1, *Tw2L, K4, Tw2R, rep from * to last st, K1.
4th row K2, * Tw2L, K2, Tw2R, K2, rep from * to end.
6th row K3, * Tw2L, Tw2R, K4, rep from * ending with K3 instead of K4.
8th row K4, * Tw2R, K6, rep from * ending with K4 instead of K6.
10th row K3, * Tw2R, Tw2L, K4, rep from * ending with K3 instead of K4.
12th row K2, * Tw2R, K2, Tw2L, K2, rep from * to end.
14th row K1, * Tw2R, K4, Tw2L, rep from * to last st, K1.
16th row K8, * Tw2L, K6, rep from * to last 2 sts, K2.
These 16 rows are repeated to form patt.

Tips

○ Choose a cable needle that is approximately the same size, or slightly thinner, than those used for knitting to avoid stretching the stitches.

○ After transferring the stitches to the cable needle, prevent a gap forming when working the next stitch on the left-hand needle by pulling the working yarn tightly across.

○ Fabrics that are heavily cabled are never lightweight due to the 'double fabric' effect created by crossing stitches. Choose suitable lightweight yarns.

Diamond lattice

(Worked over 16 sts plus 1 extra)

1st and every foll alt rows (WS) P to end.

2nd row K1, * (Tw2L) 3 times, K3, (Tw2R) 3 times, K1, rep from * to end.

4th row K2, * (Tw2L) 3 times, K1, (Tw2R) 3 times, K3, rep from * ending with K2 instead of K3.

6th row As 2nd.

8th row As 4th.

10th row K to end.

12th row K2, * (Tw2R) 3 times, K1, (Tw2L) 3 times, K3, rep from * ending with K2 instead of K3.

14th row K1, * (Tw2R) 3 times, K3, (Tw2L) 3 times, K1, rep from * to end.

16th row As 12th.

18th row As 14th.

20th row K to end.

These 20 rows are repeated to form patt.

Bobble Stitches

The raised stitches of a bobble make an unusual, highly textured fabric or design detail. Bobble stitches are often used in Aran knitting – either as a background fabric (see Trinity/Blackberry stitch, p.127) or more spaced out and combined with cables in intricate designs.

There are various methods of making a bobble: all are based on the principle of creating a number of stitches out of one, then decreasing back to the original number. The number of stitches increased and the amount of work carried out on them before decreasing determines the size of the bobble. Small bobbles are used for all-over fabrics; here a decrease immediately follows the increase, leaving a subtle texture. More pronounced bobbles are formed by turning and working several rows over the bobble stitches before reducing them to the original one.

How to Make a Bobble

This technique makes a reverse stocking stitch bobble, worked over a number of rows, against a stocking stitch background.

1 On a right-side row, knit to the position of the bobble. Working into the next stitch, knit into the front of it, then into the back alternately until there are five new stitches on the right-hand needle. Allow the original stitch to drop from the left-hand needle.

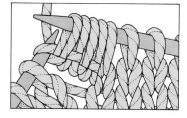

2 Turn the work so that you can continue on the five bobble stitches only. To make a reverse stocking stitch bobble, work four rows in stocking stitch (i.e. K5, turn; P5, turn; K5, turn; P5, turn).

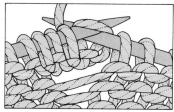

3 To decrease down to the original stitch, use the left-hand needle point to individually lift the 2nd, 3rd, 4th and 5th bobble stitches over the first one and off the needle.

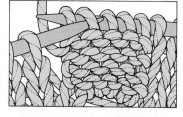

4 The right side of the work is now facing for you to continue knitting to the end of the row. After completing the bobble there will be a small hole at either side of it which is hidden by the bobble itself.

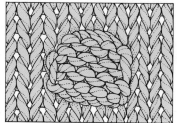

Background Fabrics

To compliment the patterned panels of Aran knitting, a plainer background is required. Most base fabrics are worked in simple stitches with a degree of texture. Reverse stocking stitch and moss stitch (see Basic Fabrics, p.51) are the most popular, but variations of moss stitch and other techniques (such as Trinity stitch, a form of bobble stitch) are also used.

Double moss stitch
(Worked over a multiple of 4 sts)
1st and 2nd rows * K2, P2, rep from * to end.
3rd and 4th rows * P2, K2, rep from * to end.
These 4 rows are repeated to form patt.

Irish moss stitch
(Worked over a multiple of 2 sts)
1st and 2nd rows * K1, P1, rep from * to end.
3rd and 4th rows * P1, K1, rep from * to end.
These 4 rows are repeated to form patt.

Trinity (Blackberry) stitch
(Worked over a multiple of 4 sts)
1st row (RS) P to end.
2nd row * (K1, P1, K1) all into next st, P3 tog, rep from * to end.
3rd row P to end.
4th row * P3 tog, (K1, P1, K1) all into next st, rep from * to end.
These 4 rows are repeated to form patt.

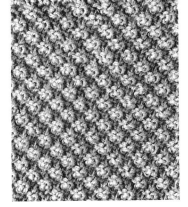

Simple Colour Effects

Although knitted fabrics comprise a wealth of interest with their decorative texture and stitches, they can be made much more exciting by the introduction of colour. The simplest way to colour a plain garment is with stripes; as long as the yarns are a similar thickness even a beginner can swiftly pick up the method.

Basic stripes in conjunction with other easy techniques can produce a variety of colourful patterns (see Slip Stitch Patterns and Chevrons, pp.132–5) that foil the eye with their complexity. For a stunning patchwork colour effect, try 'entrelacs' (see p.136). The 'plaited strips' of the fabric look very complicated, but are knitted with relative ease – all in one piece and not in separate sections as you might think.

Stripes
Horizontal stripes

Unlike substituting one stitch for another, adding stripes to a pattern does not affect the tension, so there is no need to worry about variations in size. Usually a new colour is joined in at the start of a row. To avoid darning in masses of loose ends at the end of a stripe, if the same colour is required again within a distance of 2–3cm (1in), then do not cut off the yarn. Instead carry it up the side of the work until you need it again and then resume knitting with it. Stripes generally have an even number of rows so that the yarn is always at the correct side to begin a new row.

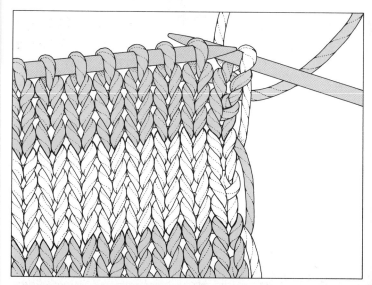

The best way of achieving a neat changeover of colours is to hold the needle with the stitches in your left hand ready to begin the next row with the new colour – one that has previously been used in another stripe. Untangle the yarns: hold the new colour in your right hand and keep any other ends clear at the back of the work. Knit the first stitch in the new colour in the usual way, keeping the loop of yarn at the right-hand edge fairly loose – pulling it tight will distort the row tension and produce an uneven result.

Simple variations

Usually stripes form a smooth, clean line on the right side of the fabric. However, there are instances when using the wrong side of the knitting, or deliberately creating texture, to give a broken stripe effect is preferable. Explore the possiblities of using simple stitches and narrow stripes to give a bright and cheerful fabric.

Each of the fabrics shown here – garter stitch, stocking stitch and moss stitch – is worked in three colours with two rows in each stripe.

Garter stitch Note that two rows in a single colour form one horizontal ridge on one side of the work. The reverse side of the fabric looks equally attractive: each horizontal ridge here is a broken stripe made with two colours.

Stocking stitch The same sequence in stocking stitch, changing colour on a knit row, gives a clean line on the right side. Broken stripes occur where you change colour on the reverse side of a stocking stitch fabric. Similar in appearance to the garter stitch version, but less textured, reverse stocking stitch has one row of solid colour separating the broken stripes.

Moss stitch The combination of knit and purl stitches creates an interesting, textured broken stripe that is the same on the back and front of the fabric.

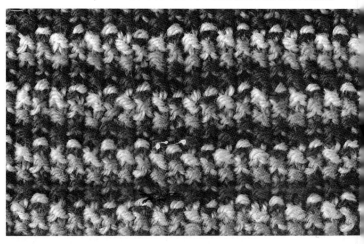

Tips

○ When adding a stripe to ribbing, knit all the stitches in the first row in a new colour to produce a clean line.

○ Use a back-stitch seam to hide the untidiness on sections where yarn is carried up the side of the work.

Narrow vertical stripes

These are not really classed as a 'simple' technique as they involve the more specialist skills of stranding generally associated with Fair Isle knitting (see pp.142–3). The stranding on the wrong side produces a fabric that is double the normal thickness, making it ideal for heavier or outdoor garments.

For a two-colour stripe sequence across a row, the yarn not in use is carried across the back of the work. It is important to keep the strands loose so that the stitch tension remains even. This method is suitable only if the stripe is no more than five stitches wide; with more stitches the strands of yarn become too long and are likely to be caught and pulled.

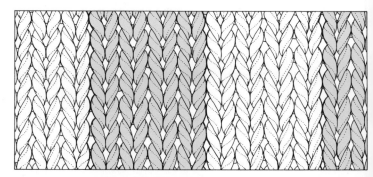

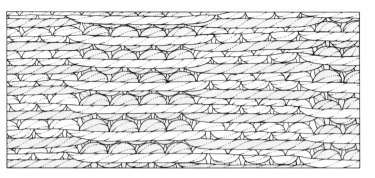

Wide vertical stripes

Again, wide stripes require the more complicated Intarsia technique (see p.147). Any number of colours can be used across the fabric as long as there is a separate ball of yarn for each stripe. At the changeover point, the colours are twisted together at the back of the work to stop them separating.

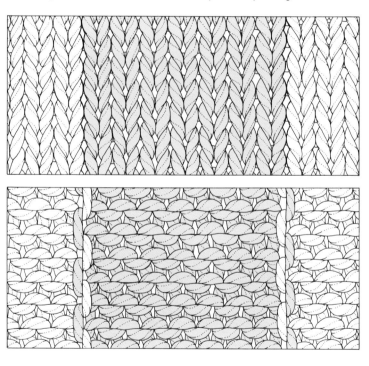

Tip

○ Striping is an ideal way of using up oddments of left-over yarn – as long as they are of a similar thickness. The same applies to entrelacs (see p.136) – each rectangular shape takes only a small amount of yarn.

Slip Stitch Patterns

For a beginner slip-stitch patterns are an easy yet extremely effective introduction to colour knitting. Using a combination of horizontal stripes and slipped stitches a two-colour effect is created across a row, but only one colour is worked at a time – the slipped stitch in a previous colour will interrupt a row being knitted in another colour.

Slip-stitch patterns are similar in looks to Fair Isle designs with a complex, multi-coloured appearance, but they are much easier to work. However, it is not always simple to substitute a slip stitch-pattern for a plain stocking stitch fabric. Slipping stitches alters the tension of the fabric by pulling the work in and drawing the rows up.

Although slip-stitch patterns are popular, you can also use garter stitch or a mixture of stitches. Add to that changes in scale from thick to thin stripes, plus more than two colours, and you will begin to see that an infinite variety of designs is possible.

The following patterns demonstrate the versatility of slipped stitches.

Note that all stitches in these patterns should be slipped purlwise. Also that on stocking stitch fabric, when slipping stitches on a knit row, you should keep the yarn at the back of the work: on a wrong-side (purl) row leave the yarn at the front when slipping a stitch.

Diagonal lines

Two colours, A and B, alternated every two rows make these staggered diagonal lines.

Using A, cast on a multiple of 6 sts + 2 extra. Using A, knit 1 row. Join in B.

1st row (RS) Using B, K1, * sl 2, K4, rep from * to last st, K1.

2nd and foll alt rows Using colour from previous row, P all sts worked in it before and sl all sts previously slipped, keeping the yarn at the front.

3rd row Using A, K3, * sl 2, K4, rep from * to last 5 sts, sl 2, K3.

5th row Using B, K1, * K4, sl 2, rep from * to last st, K1.

6th row As 2nd.

Alternating A and B every 2 rows, these 6 rows are repeated to form patt.

Mock houndstooth

A simple combination of two colours, A and B, makes this very effective houndstooth design.

Using A, cast on a multiple of 3 sts.

1st row (RS) Using A, * sl 1, K2, rep from * to end.
2nd row Using A, P to end.
3rd row Using B, * K2, sl 1, rep from * to end.
4th row Using B, P to end.
These 4 rows are repeated to form patt.

Tweed stitch

Simple garter stitch and two colours, A and B, give a small, tweed pattern. Using A, cast on a multiple of 2 sts + 1 extra.

1st row (RS) Using A, K to end.
2nd row As 1st.
3rd row Using B, * Kl, sl 1, rep from * to last st, K1.
4th row Using B, * K1, yarn to front, sl 1, yarn to back, rep from * to last st, K1.
5th–6th rows As 1st and 2nd.
7th row Using B, * sl 1, K1, rep from * to last st, sl 1.
8th row Using B, * sl 1, yarn to back, K1, yarn to front, K1, rep from * to last st, sl 1.
These 8 rows are repeated to form patt.

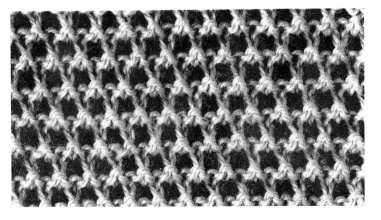

Checked pattern

In this four-colour design, colour A is always at the right-hand edge, C and D at the left-hand edge, while B travels back and forth between them. Using A, cast on a multiple of 10 sts + 4 extra.

1st row (RS) Using A, K to end.
2nd row Using A, P to end.
3rd row Using B, K1, * sl 2, K8, rep from * to last 3 sts, sl 2, K1.
4th row Using C, P1, sl 3, * P6, sl 4, rep from * to last 10 sts, P6, sl 3, P1.
5th row Using C, as 4th but K instead of P.
6th row Using B, as 3rd but P instead of K.
7th–8th rows Using A, as 1st and 2nd rows.
9th row Using B, K6, * sl 2, K8, rep from * to last 8 sts, sl 2, K6.
10th row Using D, P5, * sl 4, P6, rep from * to last 9 sts, sl 4, P5.
11th row Using D, as 10th but K instead of P.
12th row Using B, as 9th but P instead of K.
These 12 rows are repeated to form patt.

Chevron Patterns

The distinctive zig-zag pattern of chevrons is achieved by shaping the work with double decreases spaced across a row, balanced with single decreases on either side to maintain a constant number of stitches.

A number of stitches and patterns are suitable for chevrons. A successful way of highlighting the effect of a chevron fabric is with coloured stripes. The various colours are added in the same way as horizontal stripes, but the finished appearance is completely different. Follow these instructions to make a basic striped (using colours A and B) chevron fabric in stocking stitch.

Cast on a multiple of 13 sts + 2 extra.

1st row Using A, * K2, pick up loop lying between needles and K tbl (called make 1, M1), K4, sl 1 P-wise, K2 tog, psso, K4, M1, rep from * to last 2 sts, K2.
2nd row P to end.
3rd–4th rows As 1st and 2nd.
5th–8th rows Using B, as 1st–4th rows.
These 8 rows are repeated to form patt.

Note the zig-zag lower edge of the fabric as the chevrons dip at the points where stitches have been decreased and rise where they have been increased. To make deeper chevron points, work fewer stitches between the shaping positions. For example, cast on multiples of 11 stitches instead of 13, and knit three stitches (not four) at either side of the double decreases. For shallower chevrons, work more stitches between the shaping points.

Shale pattern

Chevrons are often teamed with lace patterns and stripes for a dramatic effect. Two colours are required for this pattern. Using the first colour cast on a multiple of 11 sts.

1st row (RS) * (K2 tog) twice, (yfwd, K1) 3 times, yfwd, (K2 tog) twice, rep from * to end.
2nd row P to end.
3rd row K to end.
4th row P to end.
These 4 rows are repeated to form patt, alternating the colours every 4 rows.

Garter stitch chevrons

This two-row pattern is simple to knit and is perfect for oddments of yarn.
Cast on a multiple of 14 sts + 3 extra.
1st row K1, sl 1, K1, psso, * K5, yfwd, K1, yfwd, K5, sl 2 tog K-wise, K1, p2sso, rep from * ending with K2 tog, K1 (instead of sl 2 tog, K1, p2sso).
2nd row K7, * K1 tbl, K1, K1 tbl, K11, rep from * ending with K7.
These 2 rows are repeated to form patt. Alternate the colours every 2 rows.

Entrelacs

Recently the basketweave, interlaced effect of entrelacs has been enjoying great popularity, especially as a fashion fabric. Despite being made in stocking stitch, it looks incredibly complicated because the stitches lie in different directions (not the conventional up, down and across), but in fact all the knitting is done in one piece. Colour is an important factor in entrelacs – two or more emphasize the pattern and make a novel patchwork of rectangles without the need to sew them together.

As long as you know how to decrease (see p.54), to turn rows (see p.105) and to pick up stitches (see p.62), then you can knit an entrelacs fabric.

Entrelac knitting begins with casting on sufficient stitches for all the rectangles (an even number for each). A foundation row of base triangles worked individually is knitted with turning rows, beginning with two stitches and adding one stitch every two rows. For the first row of rectangles – worked individually again – stitches are picked up from one side of a triangle; on alternate rows the work is joined to the next triangle by working one of its held stitches together with the last stitch of the present row. The top (cast-off edge) of the fabric is finished with another row of triangles worked in reverse order, while side edges require triangles at the beginning and end of rows, with a decrease at the edge on alternate rows to keep it straight.

The following instructions demonstrate an entrelacs fabric knitted in two colours (A and B), although you can add rows of colour at random.

Using A, cast on a multiple of 8 sts.

Foundation row (WS) Using A, *P2, turn, K2, turn, P3, turn, K3, turn, P4, turn, K4, turn, P5, turn, K5, turn, P6, turn, K6, turn, P7, turn, K7, turn, P8, rep from * to end. Break off A and join in B.

1st row Using B, K2, turn, P2, turn, inc in first st, sl 1 K-wise, K1, psso, turn, P3, turn, inc in first st, K1, sl 1 K-wise, psso, turn, P4, turn, inc in first st, K2, sl 1 K-wise, K1, psso, turn, P5, turn, inc in first st, K3, sl 1 K-wise, K1, psso, turn, P6, turn, inc in first st, K4, sl 1 K-wise, K1, psso, turn, P7, turn, inc in first st, K5, sl 1 K-wise, K1, psso, pick up and K8 sts down left side of triangle (or rectangle when repeating this row), working across these 8 sts and next 8sts on left-hand needle as follows: (turn, P8, turn, K7, sl 1 K-wise, K1, psso) 8 times, rep from * to last triangle, pick up and K8 sts down left side of triangle, turn, P2 tog, P6, turn, K7, turn, P2 tog, P5, turn, K6, turn, P2 tog, P4, turn, K5, turn, P2 tog, P3, turn, K4, turn, P2 tog, P2, turn, K3, turn, P2 tog, P1, turn, K2, turn, P2 tog. Break off B and join in A.

2nd row Using A and last st from previous row, pick up and P7 sts down left side of triangle and working across these 8 sts and next 8 sts on left-hand needle work as follows: (turn, K8, turn, P7, P2 tog) 8 times, * pick up and P8 sts down left side of foll rectangle, (turn, K8, turn, P7, P2 tog) 8 times, rep from * to end. Break off A and join in B.

Rep these 2 rows to form patt, ending with a 1st row.

Cast-off row *Using A and last st from previous row pick up and P7 sts down left side of triangle and working across these 8 sts and next 8 sts on left-hand needle, cont as follows: turn, K8, turn, P2 tog, P5, P2 tog, turn, K7, turn, P2 tog, P4, P2 tog, turn, K6, turn, P2 tog, P3, P2 tog, turn, K5, turn, P2 tog, P2, P2 tog, turn, K4, turn, P2 tog, P1, P2 tog, turn, K3, turn, P2 tog, P2 tog, turn, K2, turn, P4 tog, rep from * to end across foll rectangles. Fasten off.

Tips

○ Use up oddments of yarn (as long as they are the same thickness) for a colourful, entrelacs patchwork.

○ Entrelacs patterns spread when knitted. If you are devising your own fabric, make a large tension swatch to calculate the number of stitches that you need.

Fair Isle Knitting

Popularized by the Prince of Wales in the 1920s, the colourful patterns of Fair Isle knitting with their traditional quality, have become firm favourites for hand knitters: Fair Isle garments are found in many wardrobes. Fair Isle is the most southerly island of the Shetland group. The patterns traditionally known as Fair Isle (in fact, the term is now used to denote any coloured knitting where only two colours are used across a row, with the one not in use carried across the back of the work) were supposed to have been the legacy of skills taught by Spanish sailors from a shipwreck in the islands in the late 16th century.

○ The Prince of Wales playing golf at Biarritz in 1924 wearing a Fair Isle jersey.

This theory may be part of popular folklore. In reality, Fair Isle and Shetland were part of a thriving trading centre by virtue of their position on the sea route of ships crossing to Iceland in the north, America to the west, Scotland and England to the south plus Scandinavia, Germany and other destinations to the east. Knitting had long been an important livelihood.

As Fair Isle is closer to Norway than it is to the Scottish mainland, it is hardly surprising that many patterns resemble those found in Scandinavian knitting. Scandinavian designs employ the same techniques, yet they are distinctive with snowflakes and reindeer in abundance. You can identify their country of origin according to the patterns and colours – from Norway there are bold bands of design usually in a deep colour against a white background; from Denmark come smaller designs often in one colour on white; while Swedish designs are white against a grey ground. Shetland knitting is recognizable by its use of soft, neutral colours such as cream, fawn, brown and grey.

Traditional Fair Isle patterns are often symmetrical, comprising small basic motifs which are repeated to given complex designs. Knitted in stocking stitch, the patterns are usually made up of an odd number of rows, with a symmetrical design created around the central row. Although the colours used may be, or appear to be, numerous – do not be fooled. There are never more than two colours used across a single row of knitting.

Tip

○ Originally patterns were worked on circular needles so there were no problems with having the yarn ready for use at the correct end of the work. When knitting a traditional pattern you may find that the colour you need for the next row is at the opposite side of the work; cheat by slipping all the stitches from one needle on to the other. Work from the opposite end, knitting if the previous row was knitted and purling if it was purled.

Fair Isle Techniques

As a Fair Isle pattern involves working with two colours across a row, the colour not in use must be *stranded* or *woven* across the back of the work; this avoids long lengths of yarn that look ugly and catch when pulling clothes on and off.

It is vital to keep the stranding or weaving loose otherwise it is easy to alter the stitch tension. Strands that are too tight reduce the elasticity of the fabric and distort the pattern so that the stitches on the front look puckered.

Sometimes, a fabric contains a combination of techniques – both stranding and weaving. The yarn is stranded where it is applicable then, as a large gap between colours occurs, it is woven in with the central stitch (or with every third or fourth stitch, if it is a very big space).

Remember that Fair Isle work makes a double fabric which can be quite dense if the strands are woven in. Care must be taken that dark colours do not show through a light-coloured base fabric.

Working Fair Isle from a Chart

Fair Isle patterns can be given either as written instructions or in chart form. Many patterns are very long when written as row-by-row instructions, so it saves space to chart them. The other advantage of a chart is that it is so visual that you can see at a glance how the pattern should look. Charts are usually drawn on squared (graph) paper. Reading horizontally across the grid, each square represents a stitch, and vertically up the grid, squares indicate rows of knitting. The proportions of the design may look odd as graph paper is square while knitted stitches never are. If you are working out your own design, buy some ration (proportional) graph paper – especially for knitters – that shows the true shape of the stitches.

Along the right-hand side of a chart there will be a line of odd numbers – starting with 1, 3, 5, etc.: the even numbers are at the left-hand edge. These

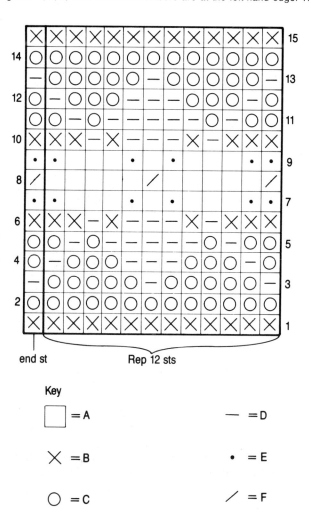

end st   Rep 12 sts

Key

☐ = A   — = D

✕ = B   • = E

○ = C   ╱ = F

numbers denote the rows in the chart. It is usual for the right-side (knit) rows to be odd numbers that are 'read' from right to left, while the wrong-side (purl) rows are even numbers that are worked from left to right.

Charts mainly show a section of the pattern that is repeated across the row. The part to be repeated is marked with strong vertical lines (that correspond to the asterisks of written instructions). Normally a row has more stitches than an exact number of repeats: these odd – edge or end – stitches are shown at either side of the repeat and may vary in number according to the size of the garment. On right-side rows, work across any end stitches at the right-hand edge once, then work across the pattern stitches repeating them as necessary before working any end stitches at the left-hand edge. Work in the reverse order for wrong-side rows.

Tip

○ Make working from a black and white chart easier on your eyes by colouring it in before you start work.

Holding the Yarns

Working simultaneously with two colours sounds difficult, but the most popular method deals with the situation well. Using *one colour in each hand* feels alien to begin with; once you get into the rhythm, it is fast and efficient. The main colour is held in your right hand and the contrast colour in your left hand, with the yarn held ready across each index finger. This method keeps the yarns from tangling, which can be a problem with stranded knitting.

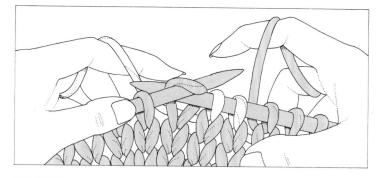

Tips

○ Make sure that the strand carried across the back of the work is loose enough for the stitches to stretch in front of it. A small loop at the back is better than pulling the strand too tightly.

○ For neat row ends always link the colour not in use in with the last stitch using the methods described in weaving.

○ When stranding colours on a purl row, you will probably find it easier to leave the contrast yarn loose – only using your left hand to actually purl a stitch.

Stranding

The yarn not in use is carried across the back of the work until it is required again. Do not bypass more than five stitches using this method. The fabric should look as neat on the back as it does on the front, with the strands loose and untwisted – one colour is always on the top and the other below it.

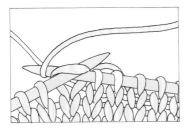

To strand the yarns across a knit row, the left hand keeps the contrast colour over to the left while the right hand knits the stitch in the usual way with the right hand.

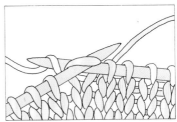

When the colours change, the right hand keeps the main colour clear while the left hand winds the contrast colour from front to back round the right needle tip. The needle tip is then used to draw a new stitch through in the contrast colour.

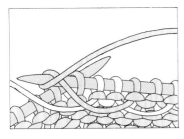

On a purl row, the left hand must keep the contrast yarn below the stitches being purled in the main colour.

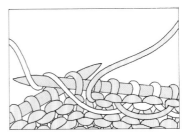

To purl a stitch in the contrast colour, the right hand keeps the main colour clear – up to the right, while the left hand winds the contrast colour right round the needle tip from the front – prior to drawing a new stitch through.

Weaving

To avoid long, loose strands when taking the yarn over long distances, use this method where the yarn not in use is looped in with the working yarn on alternate stitches, making a neat, woven effect on the wrong side of the work. Again, try to work in a relaxed way to keep the tension even.

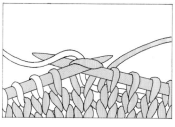

To weave in the contrast yarn (held in the left hand) on a knit row, insert the right-hand needle into the next stitch, then under the contrast colour, so looping it round the needle tip. Knit the stitch as usual, drawing the main yarn under the contrast colour to pull it through the stitch.

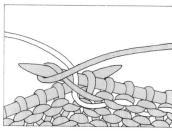

The same method applies to weaving the contrast yarn in with a purl stitch.

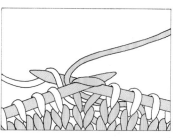

Weaving in the main yarn (held in the right hand) is more tricky. On a knit row, insert the right-hand needle into the next stitch, then wind the main colour knitwise round the needle. Position the contrast yarn round the needle tip.

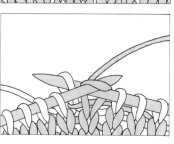

Then pass the main colour in front of the contrast and back under the right needle tip: hold it in this position as the contrast yarn is drawn through to form a new stitch.

To weave in the main colour (held in the right hand) on a purl row, insert the right-hand needle into the next stitch. Wind the main yarn under and over the right needle tip, then position the contrast colour over the needle tip ready to purl the stitch. Bring the main yarn down and under the right needle tip: the contrast yarn can now easily be drawn through to complete the stitch.

Intarsia Knitting

Intarsia is a technique used for forms of colour knitting that comprise large, independent areas of colour – such as large geometric patterns, motifs and picture knitting. There is no limit to the number of colours that can be used in a row, but the general rule is that each area of colour should have a separate ball of yarn so that colours are not carried across the back of the work as they are in Fair Isle knitting (see pp.140–2). Depending on the size of the area to be knitted, the separate yarns could be a complete ball, a smaller ball (wound on a bobbin) or just a short length.

Most intarsia work is knitted in stocking stitch to emphasize the interest in colour and design, rather than fancy stitches and texture. Other stitch patterns are used, but care must be taken that none of the twisted yarns at the back show through on the right side of the work.

Picture knit

Tips

○ Never join in a new colour with a knot. Use the method recommended on p.147.

○ Rather than knitting in very small, isolated motifs or dots of colour, it is easier to Swiss darn (see p.163) them on afterwards.

○ The finer the yarn is, the more detail you will be able to fit in; double knitting is frequently used for picture knits, 4 ply is even better.

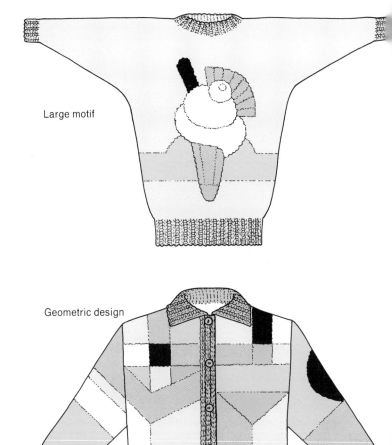

Large motif

Geometric design

Instructions for Intarsia Knitting

Instead of row-by-row instructions, charts are essential to intarsia knitting. Some advice on working from a chart is given in Fair Isle knitting (see pp.140–1): the same rules for reading the chart apply here, but there is additional information in 'picture knitting' on p.148.

In a pattern that includes single or individual motifs (rather than a repeating pattern across the fabric), the first two rows of the chart are often written out so that the motif can be positioned correctly. For example, you would be told to work until the section of garment is a certain length. To position the pattern, the instructions could read as follows: '**Next row** K34 sts using colour A, K across 20 sts of 1st row of chart using colours as required, K26 sts using colour A. **Next row** P26 A, P across 20 sts of 2nd row of chart, P34 A. These 2 rows set pattern. Continue in pattern until 18 rows have been completed.'

Twisting Yarns Together

The main point to remember about intarsia knitting is that the yarns must always be twisted together when changing colour to prevent the two sections of colour from separating completely, or to stop holes forming if the twist is missed out once or twice. The twists are always on the wrong side of the work; they must not be obvious from the front (see wide vertical stripes, p.131).

When the colour change is in a vertical line, the two colours must be twisted on every row. With a diagonal line of colour, only twist the yarns if the colour change is at the same point as the previous row. The same principle applies to twisting yarns on both knit and purl rows. Work to the position of the colour change, then pass the colour that you have finished with over the top of the new colour. Pick up the new colour and start work with it so that the thread of old colour is linked in at the point of the join.

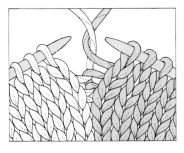

Changing colour on a knit row

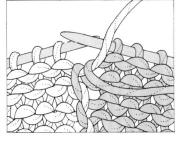

Changing colour on a purl row

Joining In a New Colour

There is no point in joining in a new colour at the end of a row with an intarsia pattern if it is not required until the middle of the row. However, to prevent a hole forming, the yarn must be joined in several stitches before it is required.

Work to four or five stitches before the colour change, then loop the new yarn over the previous one and weave it in over and under the next few stitches as you are working them. Start knitting with the new colour when it is required. Later on, you can cut off the end of yarn at the start of the weaving: unless it is required again, the other end at the finish of the colour can be darned in.

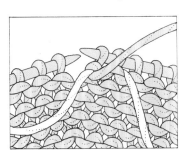

Picture Knitting

Nowadays knitted garments can become a 'canvas' for a work of art – hence the name 'picture knits'. Although the term implies the need for special techniques, none are necessary. With a stocking stitch background, the most complicated pictures can be knitted using a combination of Fair Isle and intarsia methods, with perhaps a smattering of Swiss darned embroidery. A picture uses all kinds of shapes – large and small – in the same design so the rules of applying Fair Isle or intarsia techniques are fairly flexible, but in general it is best to strand the yarns over small patterns, and where they must cross a lot of stitches, it is better to weave them in or use a separate ball of yarn.

Take care when working small areas of colour with irregular sides. If the stitch on a new row is before the position of the yarn, carrying it across will drag the stitch and spoil the outline. Ideally you must read two rows of the chart to work out if the yarn is required on the following row before the position in which it has been left hanging. Weave in the yarn until it is one stitch to the left of the point where it is to be used again. On the following row it will be one stitch to the right and can easily be drawn to the stitch being worked.

Planning a Picture Sweater

Picture knitting is always worked from a chart. It is quite possible to translate your own ideas into a picture knit – just follow the steps below for an original design. Often a picture involves all of the sweater, although usually not in so much detail as the focal point at the front. It is easiest to choose an existing plain pattern rather than trying to cope with designing a shape as well as the scene. Stocking stitch forms an ideal background for a design where the emphasis is on the pictorial representation. However, the work can be subtly enhanced using different yarns for various textures. Choose a main colour for the design that is consistent with the picture. For example, a beach scene may have three broad horizontal bands of colour – sandy yellow for the welt and lower section, sea green in the centre and sky blue for the top part and neckband.

1 Following the printed instructions for a plain sweater, mark the outline of the appropriate sections on a large sheet of graph paper (ration or proportional graph paper is best at giving a true impression of the design as it will look when knitted). Remember that a horizontal line of squares represents stitches and a vertical line represents rows. Now you can see the exact area of your 'canvas', which is useful when choosing a suitable picture.

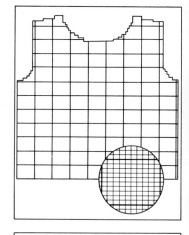

2 Draw, or trace, an existing picture on to a sheet of tracing paper using a very soft pencil. Use bold and simple outlines and think in terms of blocks of colour rather than intricate details.

3 Unless you want a mirror image of the design, turn the tracing paper and go over the lines with a soft pencil. Turn the tracing again and position it on the graph paper; retrace again so that the lines are transferred to the graph.

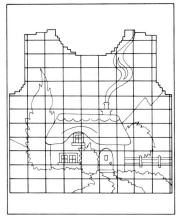

4 Translate the outlines of the sketch into squares. It is often difficult deciding exactly where the stepped outline should go – whether to include a certain square or not. Generally, if more than half of the shape appears in the square, then it should be included.

5 Block in large areas of colour on the graph paper pattern using coloured pencils lightly so that the lines of the grid are still clearly visible. Work any isolated or single stitches in the background colour and embroider them in afterwards.

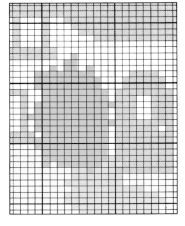

Using Bobbins

Tangled yarns can be a major problem with multi-coloured knitting. The yarns twist round one another and time is wasted sorting out the various strands at the end of each row. Where small, separate balls of yarn are required, cut-out bobbins are a solution to the tangling problem.

1 Using stiff paper or cardboard (as long as you can cut it with scissors), draw a shape as shown in the diagram, making it about 4cm (1½in) across and 5cm (2in) deep. Cut the bobbin out with a pair of scissors. Make as many bobbins as there are small, separate balls of yarn.

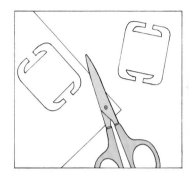

2 Wind the yarn from the main ball evenly round the centre of the bobbin until it is as full as necesary. The working end of yarn should flow from the slit at the top of the bobbin.

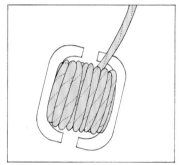

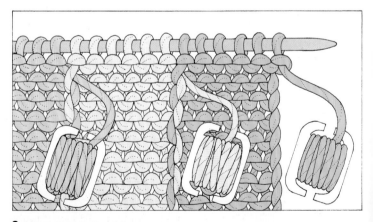

3 When working, keep the end of yarn from the bobbin fairly short to prevent it tangling with an adjacent yarn. On the wrong side of the work the bobbins hang neatly down from their respective areas of colour, without any confusion of strands.

Dropped Stitch Patterns

Very effective openwork or simulated 'lace' patterns can be created with the simple techniques of dropped stitches (of the intentional variety). One method focuses on a ladder that is formed by an intentionally dropped stitch. An increased stitch forms the platform of the ladder – either make a stitch (see p.59) or use one of the open methods of increasing (see p.154).

The following fabric shows a simple arrangement of alternating ladders against a ribbed background.

Alternating ladders

Cast on a multiple of 8 sts + 4 extra.

Foundation row (RS) K1, * P2, K1, yfwd, K1, P2, K2, rep from * to last 3 sts, P2, K1.

1st row P1, * K2, P2, K2, P3, rep from * to last 3 sts, K2, P1.

2nd row K1, * P2, K3, P2, K2, rep from * to last 3 sts, P2, K1.

3rd–4th rows As 1st and 2nd.

5th row As 1st.

6th row K1, * P2, K1, drop next st off left-hand needle and let it unravel down 6 rows to the increased st, K1, P2, K1, yfwd, K1, rep from * to last 3 sts, P2, K1.

7th row P1, * K2, P3, K2, P2, rep from * to last 3 sts, K2, P1.

8th row K1, * P2, K2, P2, K3, rep from * to last 3 sts, P2, K1.

9th–10th rows As 7th and 8th.

11th row As 7th.

12th row K1, * P2, K1, yfwd, K1, P2, K1, drop next st off left-hand needle and let it unravel down 6 rows, K1, rep from * to last 3 sts, P2, K1.

Repeat 1st–12th rows to form patt.

Lengthened Stitches

You can alter the length of a stitch by wrapping the yarn a number of extra times round the needle before working it. If you lengthen every stitch across the row by the same amount you will get a 'stripe' of long stitches.

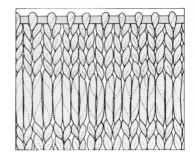

Usually the pattern tells you how many times to wrap the yarn round the right needle tip – on knit rows do this by bringing the yarn forward over the top of the needle and round to the back again (here it has been wound round twice). Then knit the next stitch in the usual way.

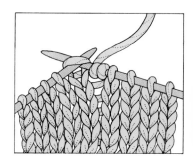

On the following row, after purling each stitch, the two extra loops just loosely wrapped around the left-hand needle tip are dropped. Note that the following stitch will be very loose when you work as it takes up the 'slack' from the extra loops.

By varying the number of times that the yarn is wrapped round the needle you can make an undulating wave pattern.

Wave pattern
Cast on a multiple of 6 sts + 1 extra.
1st row (RS) K1, * K next st wrapping yarn twice around needle – called Kw2, (K next st wrapping yarn 3 times round needle – called Kw3), twice, Kw2, K2, rep from * to end.
2nd row K to end dropping all extra loops from previous row.
3rd row K1, Kw2, K2, Kw2, * (Kw3) twice, Kw2, K2, Kw2, rep from * to last 2 sts, Kw3, K1.
4th row As 2nd.
Repeat these 4 rows to form patt.

Lace Knitting

There are several ways of forming lace patterns (also known as openwork knitting): the most usual method is making open (eyelet) increases counteracted by decreases which are not necessarily alongside, or even on the same row. Some of the most typical lace styles are really either eyelet or faggot stitch patterns depending on the position of increases and decreases. There are subtle technical differences between eyelet and faggot patterns. Generally, open increases worked on a right-side row, close to their decreases and with all alternate rows purled, are easy to work and ideal for beginners.

At the intermediate stage, vertical groupings of increases and decreases that are linked by very few strands and worked on every row, are known as lace faggot patterns. For the committed, experienced lace knitter, there are extremely lacy patterns with single threads outlining the holes and complicated repeats on both sides of the work.

The more holes that there are in a pattern, the quicker it will grow – and it will take less yarn than an average knit. Lace is often worked on larger needles than necessary to emphasize the openness; for a really lacy item, such as a shawl, it is washed and stretched (laid flat and pinned taut until it is dry) on completion to show the pattern to its best advantage. Lace fabrics have much more elasticity than other stitches. To stabilize a pattern, it is quite common to incorporate lace panels with more solid stitches at either side.

Of the wide range of yarns available, not all are suitable for lace knitting. Ideally, a lace pattern looks best in a fine, smooth yarn that is delicate and defines the stitches clearly. Fluffy yarns are possible for lace patterns as long as they are bold; stitch definition is easily blurred or 'lost' with a furry yarn.

Tips

○ When checking tension, it is easiest to measure complete pattern repeats instead of trying to count individual stitches.

○ Keep the cast-on edge loose by using the thumb method and a larger needle than stated. Alternatively, follow the special method of casting on for lace (see p.155).

○ Lace slevedges look untidy and tend to stretch. If possible, make a narrow border in a firmer stitch to make sewing up easier.

○ If a lace fabric has to be shaped (e.g. for armholes, neck, etc.) it is often impossible for patterns to print detailed instructions. To keep the pattern correct at the edges, the golden rule is to remember that any increase must be balanced by a decrease.

Making an Open Increase

An open increase, made by putting the yarn over the needle between two stitches, creates a hole when it is worked on the following row. Exactly how the yarn is placed over the needle depends on the stitches at either side – two knit stitches, a knit and a purl stitch, a purl and a knit stitch or two purl stitches.

Increasing between two knit stitches (yfwd)

At the appropriate position bring the yarn forward to the front of the work between the two needles – called 'yarn forward'. Knit the next stitch in the usual way. Notice that the yarn makes an extra loop on the right-hand needle as you wind it from the front and over the needle point. On the following row, work into each stitch as usual, including the extra loop to make a hole appear.

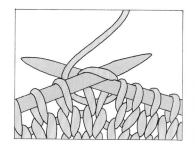

Increasing between a knit and a purl stitch (yrn)

Work to the position of the increase, then bring the yarn forward to the front between the two needles. Now take the yarn over the top of the right-hand needle point and round to the front again between the two needles – called 'yarn round needle'. Purl the next stitch in the usual way.

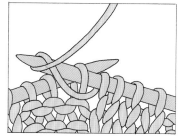

Increasing between a purl and a knit stitch (yon)

When you reach the position of the increase, you will see that the yarn is already at the front of the work from purling the previous stitch. Instead of taking the yarn to the back, as you would normally do before knitting, simply proceed to knit the stitch. As you do this, you automatically bring the yarn over the needle (yon), so creating an extra loop.

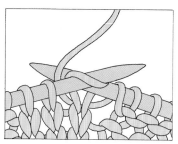

Increasing between two purl stitches (yrn)

To make a stitch between two purl stitches, take the yarn completely round the right-hand needle point and to the front again between the two needles – called 'yarn round needle'. The yarn is now in the position to purl the next stitch in the usual way.

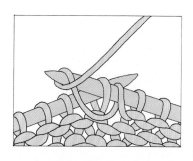

Casting On for a Lace Fabric

A lace fabric is very flexible. For a soft and supple edge try this method of casting on where the yarn is looped (rather than knitted) on to one needle.

1 Make a slip knot about 10cm (4in) from the end of a ball of yarn and place it on to a needle. Hold the needle in your right hand.

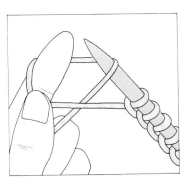

2 Wind the yarn round the index finger of your left hand as shown in the diagram, holding it in place with your thumb. Insert the needle into the loop of yarn from underneath, release your finger from the loop and tighten it on a needle.

3 You can speedily cast on the required number of stitches using this method. Take care when knitting the first row: as the stitches are not secured they can easily spring from the needle.

Casting Off a Lace Fabric

The cast-off edge of a lace fabric should be pliable in the same way as the cast-on edge. This method of casting off avoids a harsh edge which can easily happen if the individual stitches are pulled too tight.

1 Working in the usual way, work two stitches so that they are on the right-hand needle. Use the left-hand needle point to lift the first knitted stitch over the second, but leave the lifted stitch on the left-hand needle.

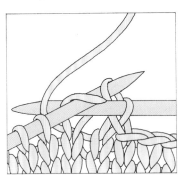

2 Now work the next stitch on the left-hand needle in the usual way and allow both loops to drop from the left-hand needle. Continue in this way until all the stitches have been cast off. You will notice that the 'suspended' stitches make a loose chain edge.

Lace Fabrics

The arrangement of open increases with decorative decreases gives infinite scope for patterned fabrics. The following are examples of popular lace patterns that are not too difficult to knit.

Cat's paw pattern

Cast on a multiple of 12 sts + 1 extra.
1st row (RS) K5, *yfwd, sl 1, K2 tog, psso, yfwd, K9, rep from * to last 8 sts, yfwd, sl 1, K2 tog, psso, yfwd, K5.

2nd and every alt row P to end.
3rd row K3, *K2 tog, yfwd, K3, yfwd, sl 1, K1, psso, K5, rep from * to last 10 sts, K2 tog, yfwd, sl 1, K1, psso, K3.
5th row As 1st.
7th row K to end.
9th row K2 tog, *yfwd, K9, yfwd, sl 1, K2 tog, psso, rep from * to last 11 sts, yfwd, K9, yfwd, sl 1, K1, psso.
11th row K2, *yfwd, sl 1, K1, psso, K5, K2 tog, yfwd, K3, rep from * to last 11 sts, yfwd, sl 1, K1, psso, K5, K2 tog, yfwd, K2.
13th row As 9th.
15th row As 7th.
16th row As 2nd.
Repeat these 16 rows to form patt.

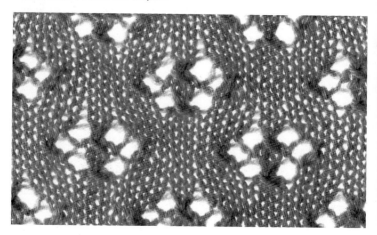

Checked mesh pattern

Cast on a multiple of 10 sts + 4 extra.
1st and every alt row (WS) P to end.
2nd row K4, *yfwd, sl 1, K1, psso, K1, (K2 tog, yfwd) twice, K3, rep from * to end.
4th row *K3, (yfwd, sl 1, K1, psso) twice, K1, K2 tog, yfwd, rep from * ending with K4.
6th row K2, *(yfwd, sl 1, K1, psso) 3 times, K4, rep from * ending with yfwd, sl 1, K1, psso.
8th row K1, *(yfwd, sl 1, K1, psso) 4 times, K2, rep from * ending with yfwd, sl 1, K1, psso, K1.
10th row As 6th.
12th row As 4th.
14th row As 2nd.
16th row K2 tog, yfwd, *K4, (K2 tog, yfwd) 3 times, rep from * ending with K2.
18th row K1, K2 tog, yfwd, *K2, (K2 tog, yfwd) 4 times, rep from * ending with K1.
20th row As 16th.
Repeat these 20 rows to form patt.

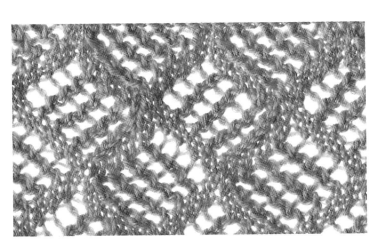

Falling leaf pattern

Cast on a multiple of 10 sts + 1 extra.

1st row (RS) K1, *yfwd, K3, sl 1, K2 tog, psso, K3, yfwd, K1, rep from * to end.
2nd and every alt row P to end.
3rd row K2, *yfwd, K2, sl 1, K2 tog, psso, K2, yfwd, K3, rep from * ending with K2 instead of K3.
5th row K3, *yfwd, K1, sl 1, K2 tog, psso, K1, yfwd, K5, rep from * ending with K3 instead of K5.
7th row K4, *yfwd, sl 1, K2 tog, psso, yfwd, K7, rep from * ending with K4.
9th row K2 tog, *K3, yfwd, K1, yfwd, K3, sl 1, K2 tog, psso, rep from * ending with sl 1, K1, psso.
11th row K2 tog, *K2, yfwd, K3, yfwd, K2, sl 1, K2 tog, psso, rep from * ending with sl 1, K1, psso.
13th row K2 tog, *K1, yfwd, K5, yfwd, K1, sl 1, K2 tog, psso, rep from * ending with sl 1, K1, psso.
15th row K2 tog, *yfwd, K7, yfwd, sl 1, K2 tog, psso, rep from * ending with sl 1, K1, psso.
16th row As 2nd.
Repeat these 16 rows to form patt.

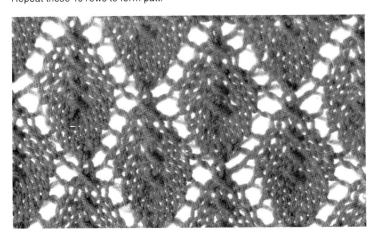

BEAD KNITTING

Bead Knitting

The traditional use of working with beads can be seen in the intricate designs from the eighteenth and nineteenth centuries when it was very popular. The knitted fabric was literally covered with beads worked on every stitch. Modern bead knitting involves placing beads at random over the fabric, or arranging them in geometric designs.

Today there is a wide choice of beads in materials such as plastic, wood or glass. Always choose beads that are a suitable weight for the fabric that you are making: you can test the size and weight by adding them to your tension square. Beads that are too big will fray the yarn; if they are too heavy, the knitting will sag. Just as important is the size of the hole – it must be large enough to thread the yarn through.

○ Bead handbags were popular accessories in the Edwardian era.

Threading Beads

Before starting to knit with beads, they must be threaded on to the yarn.

1 Cut a length of sewing thread about 15cm (6in) long. Thread both ends through a sewing needle so that a loop forms at the opposite end.

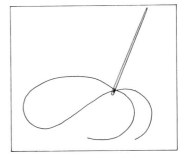

2 Pass the end of the knitting yarn through the loop and double it back.

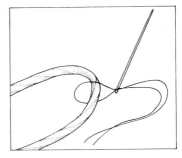

3 Hold the end of the yarn to prevent it slipping out of the thread and slip the beads on to the needle. Slide them down the needle, along the thread loop and then over the doubled yarn.

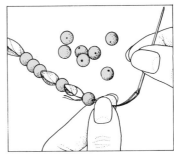

Although beads can be added at random to a favourite design, it is quite possible to knit a small, multi-coloured motif or design in beads. The design would normally be shown in the usual chart form used for knitting and it is quite easy to make up your own pattern. Decide on the area of knitting that you want to cover, perhaps marking the boundaries with pins, then count up the number of stitches and rows.

Take a piece of graph paper; using one square per stitch horizontally and one square per row vertically, mark in the design. For multi-coloured designs, represent the different beads by filling in the squares with coloured pencils; if it is a single colour or bead design you could use a symbol instead to indicate the bead positions.

Now number the rows in the direction that the chart will be read, i.e. the first row from right to left and the second from left to right. Mark alternate rows at the right side with odd numbers and the second and following alternate rows at the left edge with even numbers.

You must remember to thread the beads on to the yarn in the correct order. Basically, the last bead required for knitting is the first to be threaded on the yarn. For a design with an even number of rows, assuming that odd-numbered rows are read from right to left, start threading at the top right-hand corner, and at the left-hand corner for an uneven number of rows.

Adding Beads from the Back

If there are a lot of beads over a small area, add them from the back of the work. It is possible to bead as frequently as alternate stitches – and on alternate rows.

1 On a wrong-side row, purl to the stitch before the bead position. Insert the right-hand needle purlwise into the next stitch and wind the yarn round in the usual way. Slide a bead down the yarn until it is in position against the back of the work.

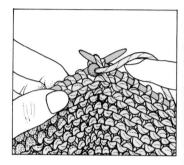

2 Purl the stitch using your left thumb to push the bead firmly through the loop and on to the right side of the work.

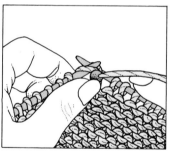

3 On the following row, secure the bead by knitting into the back of the stitch.

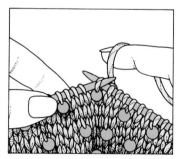

Adding Beads with a Slip Stitch

Beads knitted into the fabric (as opposite) are fully incorporated into it. When beads are added with a slip stitch they will stand clear of the surface and even hang slightly if the strand of yarn is loose. This is an ideal method for a sprinkling of beads, rather than a closely-worked motif or pattern.

1 On a right-side row, knit to the position of the bead. Bring the yarn forward to the front of the work between the needles. Push a bead down the yarn until it is in position close to the needles. Insert the right-hand needle knitwise into the next stitch.

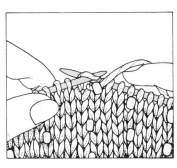

2 Slip the next stitch knitwise, making sure that the bead is in place in front of the slipped stitch. Take the yarn to the back and continue knitting to the position of the next bead.

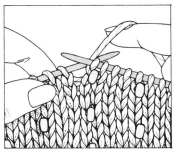

Tips

○ Make sure that beads can be washed or dry-cleaned according to the type of yarn being used.

○ If you have a large number of beads, thread a few rows at a time to make working easier. You will have more ends to darn in, but it is worth it.

○ Leave one or two selvedge stitches without beads to aid sewing up.

○ The number of beads to be threaded on to each ball of yarn is usually stated in the pattern. If this is not the case, thread one ball with more beads than you consider necessary. After knitting that ball, count the number of beads that have been used.

Embroidery on Knitting

Knitting makes a perfect base for embroidery as the horizontal lines of stitches and vertical lines of rows in a stocking stitch fabric form natural guides for work that necessitates counting out stitches. The most useful embroidery stitch to decorate knitting is Swiss darning, which is quite simple to work, but a wide range of classic embroidery stitches are also suitable. The most popular and successful stitches are shown on the following pages.

Many embroidery instructions, especially for Swiss darning, are given in chart form, usually on a squared grid. Remember that a knitted stitch is not square, so that the proportions of a finished design may be quite different.

There are a number of ways that embroidery can be worked in conjunction with knitting. Often it is added to a knitted background – for example, a Swiss darned motif – to form a complete design. Sometimes embroidery is used to highlight features of a pattern and in doing so it becomes part of the design as in Tyrolean knitting. Also embroidery is often used with other decorative techniques such as appliqué or ribbon-threading.

Using the same yarn for the embroidery as for the knitted background may be the obvious choice, but it is not the only one. Consider using embroidery yarns or tapestry threads; both are available in a large range of colours and fairly small amounts. Make sure that the embroidery yarn can be cleaned or washed in the same way as the garment and that you match the thickness of the knitting yarn, using several strands together if necessary.

Tips

- Use a soft yarn that is no thinner than the knitted background for the best results.
- Never pull embroidery stitches tight; the appearance, as well as the tension of the knitted background, will be spoilt.
- For large areas of embroidery, outline shapes with tacking.
- It is usually best to work embroidery after the knitting has been pressed, but before it is sewn up.
- Always insert the needle to the side of the stitches over which you are working a cross stitch: if you insert it through the centre, the natural elasticity of the knitting pulls the embroidery out of shape.

Swiss Darning

Added after the knitting is complete, Swiss darning resembles the knitted stitches beneath it so that it is difficult to detect that it was not knitted in. It is an ideal method for working small motifs separated by a lot of stitches (intarsia would not be suitable here) or for adding small dots or detail to Fair Isle and intarsia patterns. You can also use it to liven up an old sweater with a motif, or use the extra thickness to strengthen points that get a lot of wear such as the elbows.

Choose a yarn of equal thickness to the background so that it covers the stitch completely – a thinner yarn will not provide sufficient cover, while a thicker one will distort the fabric.

1 Thread a large, blunt-ended wool needle with yarn. Leaving a long end (to be darned in afterwards), weave the yarn in on the wrong side of the work. Bring the needle through to the right side at the base of a stitch. Working on the front of the fabric, pass the needle under both vertical threads of the same stitch, but one row above.

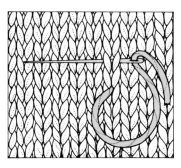

2 Re-insert the needle into the base of the first stitch and out to the front again through the base of the next stitch to the left. Avoid pulling the embroidery yarn too tightly; the darning must be kept at the same tension as the background. A V-shaped embroidery stitch has been formed covering both loops of the knitted stitch.

3 Complete a horizontal line of stitches in this way, finishing with the needle at the back of the work. To start the row above, insert the needle from back to front through the centre of the last stitch worked (if the edge is a straight line) or the centre of the stitch below the first one on the second row. It is easier to work the second and following alternate rows if you turn the knitting upside down. Now you can work the second row in the same way as the first.

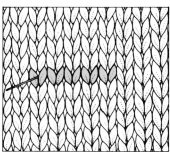

Cross Stitch

Use cross stitch on a stocking stitch background in the same way as Swiss darning – to emphasize a single stitch or for a complete motif. The lines of stitches act as guidelines. However, working on the ratio of one stitch to one row can be very fiddly and not quite in proportion (bear the proportions in mind when working a motif). Instead, cover two stitches and two rows of knitting, or three stitches and three rows, to make small and large crosses respectively.

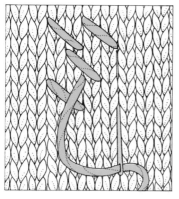

1 For an even surface to the completed embroidery, first work all the diagonal lines slanting in the same direction. Using a blunt-ended wool needle threaded with the appropriate yarn, bring it to the front at the top left-hand side of the first stitch. Re-insert the needle from front to back, diagonally opposite the corner where the yarn is joined. Continue in this way until all the stitches are worked in one direction.

2 Complete the design with the other diagonal lines worked in the opposite direction.

Lazy Daisy Stitch

Many embroidered patterns use lazy daisy stitch to form flowers. Each 'petal' of the flower is really a single chain stitch (see opposite) that can be worked large or small as necessary. Work around a central stitch, inserting the needle as shown.

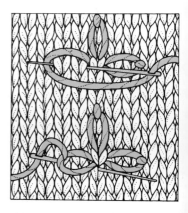

Chain Stitch

Chains are useful decorative stitches. Depending on the direction in which they are worked, diagonal chains can be used as an outline (round an intarsia shape) or as a stem in a flower pattern. Worked vertically or horizontally, they resemble the knitted stitches and can turn a plain stocking stitch fabric into a checked pattern or a striped one into a tartan.

Diagonal chains

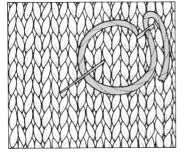

1 Thread a blunt-ended wool needle with the yarn for the embroidery. Secure the yarn at the back of the work and bring the needle from the back through to the front of the work. Form the yarn into a wide circle on top of the fabric. Holding the yarn with your left thumb, re-insert the needle at the same point and bring it to the front again at the length of the stitch (within the circle of yarn as shown).

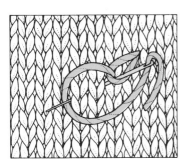

2 Pull the yarn through, drawing the large circle in to make one chain stitch. Continue to make stitches in this way until the chain is the required length. Keep the embroidery at a relaxed tension so that it does not pucker the knitted background.

3 To finish off the last stitch, insert the needle from front to back over the loop of the last chain worked and fasten off the yarn on the back of the work.

Vertical/horizontal chains

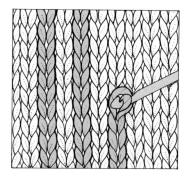

1 Use a crochet hook to draw the chain loops swiftly through the fabric. For a vertical line, commence at the lower edge and secure the yarn on the wrong side of the work. Insert the crochet hook from front to back through the centre of a knitted stitch and draw a loop through. Working through the chain loop, re-insert the hook through the centre of the next stitch (sometimes it is easier to use alternate stitches) and draw another loop through at the same time as drawing up the loop already on top of the fabric.

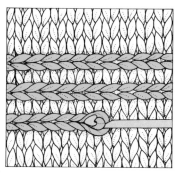

2 For horizontal chains, work in the same way as a vertical line, but across a row of stitches. Insert the hook between the stitches rather than through the centre of them.

Smocking

Ribbing is the perfect base for a smocked fabric. The smocking acts either as a decoration, say for a yoke, or as a method of gathering the fabric in. On the right side of the work, single knit 'ribs' are separated by equal numbers of purl stitches – depending on how large and deep you want the smocked honeycomb.

After the background fabric has been completed, adjacent knit ribs are joined into pairs across a row with a couple of straight stitches to anchor them. A short distance further down, the process is repeated alternating the position of the paired stitches.

Techniques for Crochet Edgings

So many patterns call for a crochet edging as a simple and effective method of neatening front edges, necklines and openings that it is worth mastering a few basic crochet skills. At first holding the yarn and hook for crochet will probably feel unfamiliar. The following diagrams show how the yarn is wound round the fingers of the left hand with it loosely anchored round the little finger (the yarn must always be allowed to flow by moving the fingers) while the index finger controls the flow. The right hand holds the crochet hook as shown here. For a crochet fabric, the first loop on the hook is always a slip knot: for an edging this first stitch is worked through the fabric.

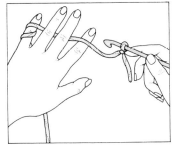

Yarn wound round left hand

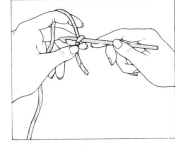

Holding the hook

Double crochet edging

This is the most popular crochet edging. The crochet stitches are worked over the knitted edge to make a neat chain finish that is solid and will not stretch.

1 With the right side of the edge to be worked along facing upwards, tie the yarn being used to the first stitch below the 'chain' edge. Insert the crochet hook from front to back into the same place as the yarn and wind the yarn in a clockwise direction around the hook.

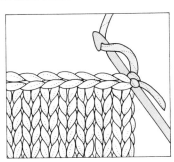

2 Draw the hook and yarn through to the front so that there is one stitch on the hook. Wind the yarn around the hook again and draw it through the stitch on the hook to secure the first stitch.

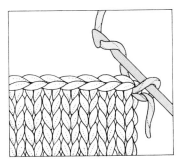

continued

3 Insert the hook from front to back under both chain loops of the next stitch along. Wind the yarn round the hook as before and draw through a loop so that there are two loops on the hook. Wind the yarn around the hook and draw it through both loops to complete one double crochet stitch.

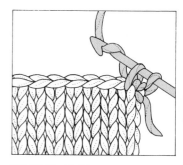

4 Continue along the edge, repeating step 3, so that one double crochet is worked into each stitch. To fasten off, cut the yarn leaving an end and draw it through the loop on the hook.

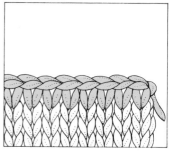

Crab stitch
Another popular edging with a corded appearance, crab stitch is worked in double crochet *but* in a left to right direction instead of from right to left.

Join in the yarn at the left-hand edge of the work and continue as given for a double crochet edging (above). Even if you are an experienced crochet worker you will find it strange to be doing familiar actions 'back to front'; it is only after you have worked for some way that the attractive edging becomes apparent.

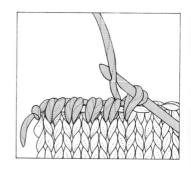

Slip stitch edging
A crochet slip stitch is very shallow and unobtrusive. It makes a neat, subtle finish that is useful for tightening edges (do not work into every stitch).

Work the first two steps as given for a double crochet edging. Insert the hook from front to back under one (or two) loops of the next stitch along. Wind the yarn round the hook and draw it through *both* loops on the hook to complete one slip stitch. Continue in this way for the required distance.

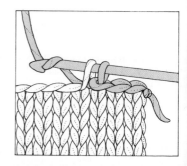

Correcting Mistakes

All knitters make mistakes: correcting them is very good practice especially for new knitters who will probably be using these techniques more than others. No matter how serious the mistake, it is vital not to panic. With a calm approach you have a much better chance of sorting out the problem. Mistakes fall into two categories – minor and major. Minor mishaps include dropped stitches, extra (unwanted) stitches, twisted stitches and mistakes in the pattern. Major errors are luckily quite rare, but would include noticing a glaring mistake some distance back in the work. However hard you try to convince yourself that it will not show – the fact is that it probably will. In this situation the only answer is to unravel the work back to the mistake. What do you do with unravelled yarn (apart from using it to finish the garment that you are making)? Recycle it – see p.172 for further details.

Tips

○ Keep checking your work for dropped stitches: it saves time later.

○ Keep safety pins to hand to hold dropped stitches and prevent them travelling further.

○ Take prompt action – stop a dropped stitch as soon as you see it by holding it on one of the needles.

○ When picking up a dropped stitch that has run down several rows on a stocking stitch fabric, you will find it easiest to do with the knit side of the fabric facing you.

Small Mistakes

Complicated techniques are unnecessary to deal with minor errors – such as twisted stitches, extra stitches or mistakes in the pattern – that are confined to one stitch. Continue with the row that you are working up to the stitch that is immediately above the error. Drop the next stitch and allow it to run down to the row below the error, then trap it on a safety pin. Repair the ladder as given for dropped stitches 'several rows below' on p.171.

Dropped Stitches

Hopefully you will quickly spot a dropped stitch – either on the row being worked, the row below or a few rows down – and so be able to remedy it promptly. Further than a few rows down can be difficult particularly if the tension is tight. With a loose tension, the dropped stitch can be worked several rows up the 'ladder' because the surrounding stitches have sufficient ease to cope with the new stitch. If the stitch drops more than two rows down on a tight fabric, it is best to unravel back to that point rather than risk a tight, puckered effect.

On the row in progress

You may notice a dropped stitch as you are working before it starts to run down the rows so creating a ladder. If necessary unravel the row back to the dropped stitch, then replace it on the left-hand needle making sure that it is not twisted.

One row below – rescuing a knit stitch

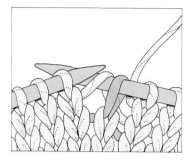 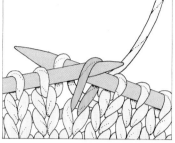

1 Insert the right-hand needle into the dropped stitch from *front* to *back* and then under the horizontal strand of yarn so that it lies *behind* the stitch.

2 Insert the left-hand needle point into the *front* of the dropped stitch from *left* to *right* and lift it over the strand of yarn and off the needle as though casting off. Replace the stitch on the left-hand needle by inserting the needle point from *front* to *back* through it.

Rescuing a purl stitch

1 Insert the right-hand needle into the dropped stitch from *back* to *front* and then under the horizontal strand of yarn so that it lies *in front* of the stitch.

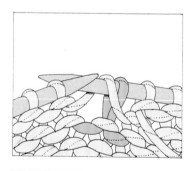

2 Insert the left-hand needle point into the *back* of the dropped stitch from *left* to *right* and lift it over the strand of yarn and off the needle. Replace the stitch on the left-hand needle by inserting the point from *back* to *front* through it.

Several rows below

As the stitch unravels down the fabric, it leaves a ladder of horizontal strands of yarn each representing a row. You can work the stitch up the ladder, row by row, following the instructions for a stitch that has dropped one row below.

Alternatively you can use a crochet hook in a finer size than the needles to swiftly take the stitch up the ladder.

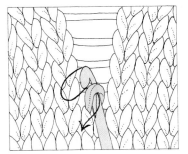

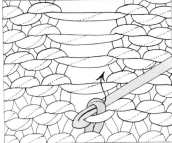

Rescuing a knit stitch

Insert the crochet hook into the dropped stitch from *front* to *back*. With the hook pointing up, use it to catch the first horizontal strand of yarn from above and draw it through the dropped stitch. Continue to repeat this action until the stitch is level with the row being worked, then replace it on the left-hand needle.

Rescuing a purl stitch

Insert the hook into the dropped stitch from *back* to *front*. With the hook pointing *down*, use it to catch the first horizontal strand of yarn from above and draw it through the dropped stitch. The hook is now inserted into the front of the stitch. To repeat the actions up the ladder, remove the hook from the stitch each time and replace it from *back* to *front*.

Unravelling Work

However careful you are with your knitting, there are bound to be occasions when the only solution to a problem is to undo the work. Exactly how you unravel stitches depends on the position of the mistake.

Unravelling a single knit row

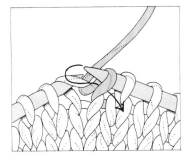

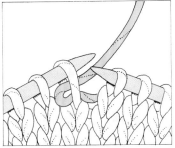

1 Holding the work as usual with the stitches to be unravelled in your right hand, insert the left-hand needle point from *front* to *back* through the centre of the stitch *below* the first one on the right-hand needle.

2 Allow the stitch to fall from the right-hand needle. Pull the working yarn to unravel the stitch. Repeat these actions stitch by stitch.

Unravelling a single purl row

Follow the same instructions as for unravelling a knit stitch.

Unravelling a large section

If you notice a glaring error in your work some way back, then it is tedious and impractical to unravel it stitch by stitch, row by row. You must remove the work completely from the needles and pull the stitches undone. Hold the work firmly in one hand, gathered up to prevent ladders, and pull the yarn to unravel it with the other hand. Smooth yarns are easiest to undo; brushed or hairy ones will probably stick now and again and may require some coaxing.

The main worry for most knitters when using this method is how to retrieve the stitches after the unravelling is finished. The best way is to leave the last row to be undone intact, then work across it slowly unravelling a few stitches at a time and replacing them on the needle.

Do not worry if you discover the stitches are twisted on the needle; as you come to a twisted stitch, you can either straighten it on the needle or work it through the back of the loop.

Recycling Yarn

Are you taking a garment apart (perhaps you are fed up with a knit that has been lurking in a cupboard) or do you have long-forgotten pieces of unfinished knitting? If you decide to have a clear out, then there is no need to waste the yarn – it can be recycled.

Any yarn that you want to re-use must be in good condition and will need to be unravelled. If the knitted fabric has felted, it will be difficult to unravel the stitches. You will probably be restricted to using fairly plain yarns as many fashion yarns are too textured or hairy to unwind successfully. Even yarn that has been knitted for a short time is crinkled. Unless you are just undoing a section of garment you are working on to correct an error and intend to re-use the yarn immediately, it must be treated to smooth it.

1 Using a board or chair back, wind the unravelled yarn back into a skein. Secure the two ends with a large, loose knot. Tie the skein in three or four places using tape or very strong yarn.

2 Following instructions, wash the skein and rinse, but do not wring out the water. Hang the dripping skein, pegged to the line by one of the ties, to dry away from direct sun and heat. Attach a weight to the lower edge to aid the weight of the water in pulling the yarn taut as it dries. When the yarn is dry, wind it loosely into a ball.

Making Up a Knitted Garment

The importance of the final stages of making a knitted garment, including pressing, assembling the various pieces and joining them together, can not be over-estimated. For a professional finish you must take care with the making up: it should not be rushed. If you consider the number of hours spent in actually knitting the garment, then it would be a waste of time and effort if the final effect was marred by shoddy assembly.

First check the pieces of fabric for mistakes while there is still time to remedy them: you can always re-knit a section as a last resort at this stage. Then see that all the pieces fit together as intended with equal front and back armhole depths, and side seams that correspond in length.

Before making up any garment, check the ball bands and pattern leaflet for instructions on pressing. A list of symbols that you are likely to encounter on a ball band is shown on pp.154–5. In general yarn with a high wool content needs pressing with a warm iron over a damp cloth to even out the stitches. Many synthetic yarns do not need pressing; should it be necessary, it is best to use a cool iron over a dry cloth. Textured or fluffy yarns and raised stitch patterns can be flattened and ruined by pressing. Instead, they should be damp finished.

Blocking

This is the process of preparing the individual pieces of knitting, before sewing them up, by setting them to the required size and shape. Adjusting any discrepancies in size is easy to do at this stage. The knitted fabric is so elastic that it can be stretched or reduced by careful blocking and pressing.

1 Prepare a padded surface on which to pin out the knitted pieces. Place a folded blanket on a table or ironing board and cover it with a clean cloth. Lay the section of garment down with the wrong side facing upwards and smooth it out to the correct measurements.

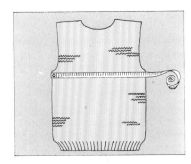

2 Check that the lines of stitches and rows lie correctly both horizontally and vertically before placing pins through the knitted edge – at right angles to it – and into the padded surface. Keep the pins at fairly frequent intervals so that a smooth outline is achieved. Do not pin or press any ribbed sections.

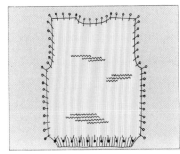

Pressing

Use a pressing cloth – damp or dry, depending on the yarn (see opposite) – to cover the knitting. Check that the iron is at the correct setting, then move it from section to section by lifting it directly up and placing it down in the same way. Do not press any areas of ribbing or garter stitch. Now, leave the knitting to dry completely before removing the pins.

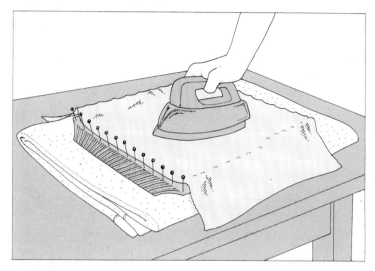

Damp Finishing

Try this method of finishing for yarns or patterns that would be damaged by pressing. Make up the garment as instructed in the pattern. Roll up the finished garment in a wet, colourfast towel. Leave it to absorb the moisture (approximately one hour). Unwrap the garment and lay it out on the damp towel placed flat on a surface.

Ease the garment into shape, checking the measurements as described in 'blocking' (see p.173). Use a second damp towel to cover the knitting and leave everything in place to dry naturally. Do not remove the knitted garment until it is completely dry.

Sewing Up

There are many types of seam used in knitting: choose one that is suitable for the job. The seams described here are the most popular and can be used in the majority of cases. Always use a blunt-ended wool needle to avoid splitting the stitches and thread it with the same yarn as the garment. Use the ends of yarn from the knitting if they are in the correct position. If the yarn is very thick, it is usually possible to separate the plys to make thinner strands for sewing. For textured or fluffy yarns choose a smooth yarn in a matching colour (as long as it can be laundered in the same way as the main garment). Complete the seam with two small stitches, then darn in the yarn for several centimetres before cutting it off.

Backstitch Seam

Probably the most popular seam in common use, the backstitch seam gives a strong, firm finish to most edges so making it very useful where they are uneven, such as at the shoulder seams. As the line of stitching is worked one stitch in from the edge, do not use this seam on very thick fabrics or the finished seam will be too bulky.

1 Pin the pieces to be joined with right sides together, matching the edges. Use a double stitch to start off with, enclosing the ends of the seam for strength.

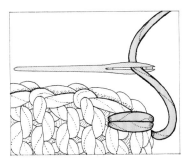

2 Make a running stitch no more than 1cm ($\frac{3}{8}$in) long and push the needles through the fabric from the back to the front: pull the thread through. Re-insert the needle at exactly the same place as before and bring it through to the front the length of a stitch further on; pull the thread through.

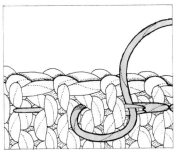

3 Re-insert the needle at the end of the first stitch and bring it through to the front again another stitch length on. Continue in this way, keeping the stitches uniform and the seam straight. On the side that you are working there must be no gaps between the stitches.

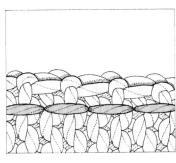

On the reverse side, the stitches overlap one another.

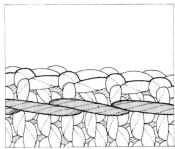

Overcast Seam

This is also known as a flat seam. Although the work is done through two edges placed together, when it is opened out the seam lies completely flat. Use an overcast seam for heavy yarns and areas of ribbing on a garment such as welts and cuffs. It is a particularly useful and neat method of attaching front bands (see p.66) or collars (see p.78).

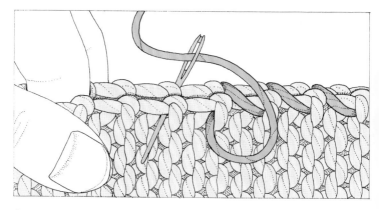

1 On a stocking stitch fabric, place the edges to be joined with right sides together and matching row ends. For ease, work with your index finger between the two fabrics; pin the seam some distance away to allow space for your finger. After joining in the yarn, insert the needle behind the knot of the edge stitch on one piece, then through the same part of the corresponding stitch on the second piece. Draw the yarn through and repeat these actions to join each pair of row ends. Always use the 'knot' of the stitches, rather than the strands between the rows, as a base for the seam because it is the strongest part of the stitch.

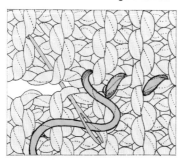

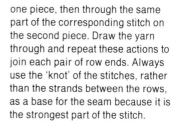

2 For a garter stitch fabric, thread the needle through the *bottom* of the stitch on one side, then through the *top* of the corresponding stitch on the second side. When the seam is opened flat, the line of stitching is virtually invisible and does not interrupt the lines of garter stitch.

Tips

○ Do not take a complete edge stitch into the seam or it will be too lumpy and uneven when opened out.

○ Although the section you are working on requires a different type of seam, it is still possible to start with an overcast seam for the ribbing, then change to the correct seam afterwards.

Invisible Seam

Also known as ladder stitch seam or mattress stitch seam, this is the method that many professional knitters prefer for a perfect finish. The seam is most suitable for unshaped stocking stitch fabrics where the number of rows tally exactly. It is easy to see exactly what you are doing as the pieces are placed edge to edge and then 'laced' together from the *right* side of the work. On completion the join is undetectable from the right side both in looks and by feel – the only sign of the seam is a slight ridge on the inside of the garment.

1 With the right side of both pieces of work facing upwards, join in the yarn and thread the needle under the horizontal strand (linking the edge stitch and following stitch) of two stitches. Draw the yarn through to the right side. Now insert the needle through the same two strands on the second edge.

2 Continue in this way, working under two strands at alternate edges. The thread 'laces' the work together; draw it up gently at regular intervals to pull the seam together.

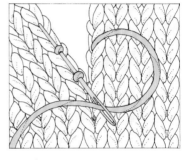

Tips

○ Use long pins with coloured heads as they are easy to handle. You can also quickly distinguish them in the knitted fabric.

○ To dampen the knitting use a fine plant spray.

○ When pressing, never push the iron over the knitted surface.

○ Work that has been flattened by over-pressing can be improved by steaming. Hang the garment so that the steam from a boiling kettle can circulate round it.

○ If the knitted fabric is very thick, insert the needle under *one* horizontal strand each time not *two* as specified.

Remodelling Garments

There are a number of reasons why you may need to alter an existing garment – including adapting the size (maybe to suit a growing child), changing a damaged area or re-styling an out-of-date garment. You can also liven up a classic garment: a crew neck sweater becomes a tunic style when you lengthen it and add trimmings such as a collar, pocket top and hankie. If it is impossible to obtain yarn in the correct shade for lengthening, add contrast-coloured stripes.

Horizontal adaptation such as lengthening and shortening is the easiest. The fabric must be 'cut' following the methods described here. Although it is possible to cut knitting in the ordinary way, this is a drastic step that is not generally recommended unless undertaken by an expert.

Original garment

Remodelled garment with new collar, pocket and lengthened body

Altering the Length of Existing Knitting

To lengthen or shorten a knitted fabric, never simply cut the knitting. Unpick the seams and divide the fabric as shown. First select the best position for altering the length. A sweater needs extra length added or subtracted two or three rows above the welt or cuff.

Lengthening

1 Unpick any seams to about 5cm (2in) above the adjustment point to give you freedom to manipulate the needles when you re-knit. Insert the point of a knitting needle into a stitch (two stitches in from the right-hand edge) and use it to loosen the stitch. Use your thumb and forefinger to pull the stitch into a long, loose loop. As you draw the loop up, the other stitches in the row tighten across the width of the fabric, leaving a hard, horizontal ridge on the back of the work.

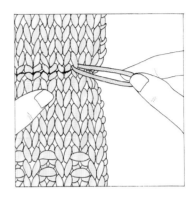

2 Cut the loop and gently pull the fabric apart at the right-hand edge until the loops of two or three stitches are free. Use the point of a knitting needle to draw one cut end of yarn through each stitch individually to unravel the stitches.

3 Continue in this way until the two sets of stitches are exposed. (Do not discard the lower section: the number of rows in it must correspond to those knitted *after* inserting the extra length.) Pick up the stitches at the lower edge of the main piece. With the wrong side of the work facing, start at the left-hand edge and insert the knitting needle from front to back through the first stitch. Continue to pick up all the stitches in this way. Starting with a wrong-side row, knit in a downwards direction – first adding the extra length, then working the rows at the top of the welt and finally the ribbing. Cast off for the lower edge. Despite knitting downwards, the stitches lie in the same direction as before, making the join undetectable.

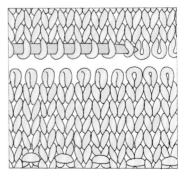

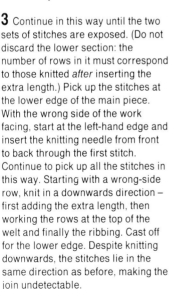

Shortening

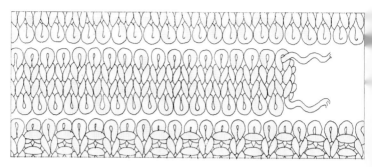

1 Divide the fabric in *two* places in the same way as described for lengthening. The section between the divisions must be equal to the amount that needs to be shortened. If the edges are to be grafted together, the section must be taken out of an area with no shaping so that you are left with the same number of stitches on the edges to be grafted. Remove the unwanted section leaving two sets of loops exposed – those at the lower edge of the main section and those just above any ribbing or hem.

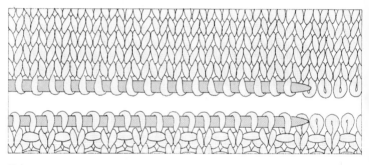

2 Pick up the stitches so that the needles are pointing in the same direction. For an invisible join, graft the two sections together.

Tips

○ If you envisage altering a garment at a later stage, it is worth buying extra yarn in the same dye lot at the outset.

○ Seam stitches are difficult to detect in knitted fabric. If you anticipate unpicking a seam, run a length of fine thread in a contrasting colour together with the stitches to indicate the position of the seam.

○ Unless you are very confident, only alter the length of sections of garment without shaping.

○ Practise these techniques first with fabric samples.

○ Do not attempt grafting heavily-textured yarns; they will not thread easily through the stitches.

Grafting

This is a method of joining two sections of knitting with a blunt-ended sewing needle. Instead of a seam, the join is invisible as the needle and thread exactly imitate the path of the knitted stitch. The technique is mainly successful with basic stitches; it works best when used with the knit stitches on the right side of stocking stitch.

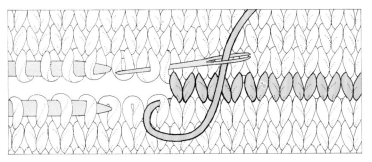

1 Lay the two pieces of knitting on a flat surface with the needles together and pointing in the same direction – to the right. To avoid laddering, slip two or three stitches off the needles at a time or as required. Using the same thread as the background fabric, secure it at the back of the work and insert the needle from *back* to *front* through the first lower loop.

2 Thread the needle from *front* to *back* through the first upper loop, then from *back* to *front* through the next upper loop. Insert the needle from *front* to *back* through the first lower loop, then from *back* to *front* through the next lower loop. Repeat from this step, making sure that you always work twice through each loop.

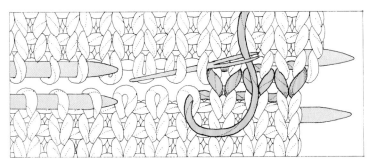

To graft together two pieces of single rib you will require four extra double-pointed needles so that the knit and purl stitches can be split and worked separately. On both sections of rib use one double-pointed needle to hold the knit stitches and another for the purl stitches. With the right side of the work facing, graft the knit stitches from two opposite needles together as given for stocking stitch (see above). Afterwards turn the work and graft the stitches from the remaining two needles, again in a knitwise direction.

MENDING

Mending

It is not uncommon to become very attached to your knitteds, especially if you have spent painstaking hours in making them. Therefore it is not surprising that hand-knitted garments do not easily fit in with our image of a modern, throw-away society. The urge to mend and care for knitted garments makes sound sense.

The most frequent problems due to wear or accidents involve holes and pulled threads. Your most valuable asset on these occasions is some of the original yarn. Even your tension swatch (which should be filed away) can be unravelled and used if you are desperate.

Holes

Small

Providing that the hole is no deeper than one row and that the fabric is fairly plain, then the edges can be grafted together (see p.181). After undoing any damaged stitches, you can use spare yarn to graft the exposed sets of loops together so that the join is virtually undetectable. Leave sufficient of the original yarn at either end of the join to secure in with the grafting yarn.

Large

The most difficult problem in the case of large holes – where a section of knitting over a number of stitches and rows has been damaged – is the exposed sets of row ends which must be secured as soon as possible. Sometimes the hole can be repaired by grafting in a knitted patch as long as it is not in an area of the garment that is subjected to strain, such as the elbows. First remove the damaged yarn by carefully unpicking it to leave a neat hole with the same number of exposed loops along the top as there are at the lower edge. Loosely knot the row-end threads together to prevent further damage.

Using the loops from the lower edge of the hole and the original needle size, work the same number of rows that are missing. Finally, graft the last row together with the loops at the top of the hole. Sew down the side edges using an overcast seam (see p.176): carefully secure the row-end threads as you are stitching.

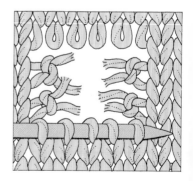

Patching

In some instances, such as where none of the original yarn is available or if a stitch pattern in not suitable for grafting, a knitted or fabric patch can be be sewn on to cover the hole. First strengthen the area and prevent the hole from growing larger by stitching on the garment, preferably by machine, the shape of the patch, but slightly smaller so that it will be concealed when the patch is in place. Work more criss-cross lines over the stitching to form a solid base for the patch. Once the patch has been sewn in position neaten the back by sewing the raw edges of the hole to the patch.

Pulled Thread

Knitted fabric that has been caught on something sharp often forms loops of yarn, where a stitch has been pulled, that hang loose on the right side of the work. The stitches in the same row as the pulled thread are usually drawn tight as a result of this action.

If the loop is relatively small you may be able to gently tug the surrounding fabric and ease it back into place. Otherwise, use a cable needle or a blunt-ended sewing needle and, starting at the end of the row furthest from the pull, ease the yarn along from one stitch to another. By the time you arrive at the pulled thread, the loop should have reduced sufficiently for you to tug it into place.

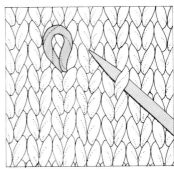

Occasionally if the loop is very long or broken it may be necessary to take it through to the back of the work using a crochet hook. Tie the cut ends together to prevent any dropped stitches, then try easing the yarn along as before. Afterwards the knotted ends must be undone and secured into the fabric.

Tips

○ Take the garment with you if you need to buy new yarn – shades are notoriously difficult to match.

○ Disguise a small hole with Swiss darning if it is compatible with the fabric and the style of garment.

Washing and Storing

The whole process of making a knitted garment takes a lot of care, time and work, but the end result is usually well worth the effort. Now, the completed garment deserves special attention that will guarantee it many years of serviceable life in your wardrobe. Learn how to treat your knitteds and you will never know the disappointment of finding your favourite sweater transformed into a felted, shrunken, holey, totally unwearable horror.

Washing

Hand knits need to be washed fairly frequently before they become heavily soiled. Dirt can break the delicate fibres and spoils the appearance of the garment. Always consult the yarn ball bands for laundering details. The symbols here are part of an international coding system that is in common use.

Many yarns today are machine-washable. Either the term 'superwash' in the name of the yarn or the symbols on the ball band indicate whether this is so. Even if you do put your knitteds in a machine they must be washed on a wool programme.

If you are in any doubt about the correct method of laundering, it is always safest to wash the garment by hand. In fact, hand-washing is often the only way to treat delicate fibres and patterns.

TYPE OF CARE	DRY CLEANING	WASHING
Fairly easy care	(A) Use any dry-cleaning fluid	6 / 40° Can be machine-washed at stated temparature
Treat carefully	(P) Use perchlorethylene or white spirit only	30° Recommended water temperature for hand washing
Handle with great care	(F) Use white spirit only	Wash by hand only
Do not use treatment shown	⊗ Must not be dry-cleaned	Must not be washed

The main problems associated with washing involve shrinking and stretching. Shrinking and a felted fabric occurs when wool (or a wool mixture) is washed at too high a temperature with excessive friction. Synthetic fibres are more prone to stretching: unless they are handled carefully the weight of water absorbed by a garment during washing pulls it out of shape.

Typical labels for hand-washable
garments and yarns

	HAND WASH ONLY
6	Warm (40°C) Cold rinse
	Spin Do not hand wring

	HAND WASH ONLY
7	Warm (40°C) do not rub
	Spin Do not hand wring

	MACHINE	HAND WASH
6	Warm (40°C) minimum wash	Warm (40°C)
	Cold rinse Short spin Do not wring	

	MACHINE	HAND WASH
7	Warm (40°C) minimum wash	Warm (40°C) Do not rub
	Short spin Do not hand wring	

BLEACHING	DRYING	IRONING
Chlorine (household) bleach may be used	Can be tumble dried	High setting — hot
	Dry on a line	Medium setting — warm
	Allow to drip dry	Low setting — cool
Do not use household bleach	Do not hang — lay flat	Must not be ironed

Hand Washing

1 Use a special powder or solution for hand washing delicate fabrics, never an ordinary washing powder. Completely dissolve the preparation in warm water, then add sufficient cold water to make it lukewarm.

2 Immerse the garment in the suds and work quickly, using your hands to expel soapy water by gently squeezing – never wringing. Do not add more washing solution at this stage.

3 Carefully lift the garment out of the water, supporting it with both hands. Now rinse the garment in water of the same temperature; you may need to do this several times until the water becomes clear. After rinsing, squeeze as much water as possible from the garment, but do not wring it – support it in a bowl or on a draining surface until you are ready to transfer it for drying.

Tip

○ If you are in any doubt about how your knitting will react to washing, use your tension swatch as a test piece.

Drying

The nature and quality of the yarn dictates the use of spin and tumble dryers (always check the ball bands to see what is recommended). Spin drying is an excellent way of getting rid of excess moisture: it is ideal for woollens, especially large, bulky items. However, never put a woollen garment in a tumble dryer as the heat felts the fabric.

Leave synthetic fibres until they are cold before giving them a short spin dry; they become distorted and creased if spun whilst warm. On the other hand, synthetics may be tumble dried quite successfully if you remove them from the machine before they are fully dry and leave them flat to finish drying.

The following steps demonstrate the important points to remember when drying knitted garments, especially if spin and tumble dryers are unavailable.

1 Remove as much water as you can from the garments as quickly as possible. Gently squeeze the knitted between towels to prevent it being pulled out of shape. Never twist or wring water out of knitting. Prepare a flat surface for drying: pad it with newspaper covered with a large, colourfast towel.

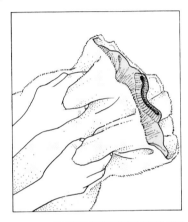

2 After lightly shaking the garment to even out the stitches, lay it on the drying surface and gently re-shape it back to its original size, smoothing out any creases. Use a tape measure to check that the original main measurements – around the chest, length and sleeve seam – are correct. Leave the garment until all the excess moisture has been absorbed by the towel and newspaper; never lift it up until it is completely dry.

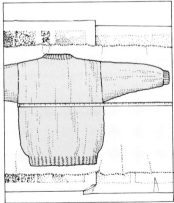

Tips

○ Never hang knitting up to dry.

○ Slatted, or mesh, drying frames are useful for drying knitting as they keep the garment flat, yet allow the air to circulate all around.

Stains

Prompt action on the discovery of a stain may avoid the necessity for washing or dry cleaning. First try dabbing or sponging – do not rub – the work with cold water; if applied soon enough this may solve the problem. Water must not be used for oil-based stains such as make-up, ball pen or grease: instead they must be treated with a solvent applied to the wrong side of the fabric. The stain will be forced out of the fibres and onto a clean white cloth held against the right side of the knitting. Even if a mark has been undetected for a while and laundering is inevitable, treat it first to loosen the stain. Dab the blemish with a solution of equal parts of glycerine and warm water and leave to soften for about an hour. Then rinse with lukewarm water and launder as appropriate.

Dry Cleaning

If washing your hand knit is impossible, or you want to remove any element of risk that it might be damaged, dry cleaning is a perfectly acceptable method of laundering, unless the ball band specifically forbids it. Garments that have been dry-cleaned keep their shape, colour and texture better than those which have been washed. However, choose a reputable shop: a lingering solvent smell can be a problem if the fluid is not changed regularly. If the garment must not be pressed or hung up, then remember to give the appropriate instructions when you take it in for cleaning.

Storing

One of the most common fates of knitted garments, causing irreparable damage, is hanging them up for storage. Ends of coat hangers or hooks make unsightly distortions in the fabric at the shoulders or back of the neck. Also the elasticity of the fabric means that most garments, especially if they are big and bulky, stretch downwards.

When a garment is thoroughly dry, it should not require pressing if it has been smoothed and flattened correctly during the drying process. If you think that pressing would improve the look, first check with the original ball band to choose the correct method.

Before storing a knitted sweater or jacket in a closed polythene bag laid on a shelf, fold the garment as shown opposite. If the storage area is cold, do not wrap the garment in a bag; instead keep the area well aired.

Tips

○ Never hand wash more than one item at a time unless they are very small.

○ Never dry a woollen garment outside in direct sunlight – it can scorch!

○ Put delicate machine-washable knits in a pillow slip to prevent damage and stretching during washing.

○ Damp wool is very pliable. Before drying, you can gently stretch a garment or coax it into a smaller shape.

○ Store newly washed knitting in a warm atmosphere.

○ Remember that only clean knitting should be stored for any length of time.

Folding a Garment

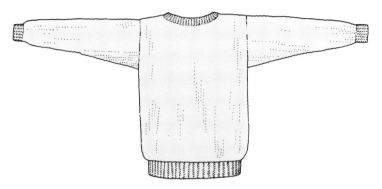

1 Lay the garment face down on a flat surface with both sleeves fully extended.

2 Fold in one sleeve diagonally with the side of the garment.

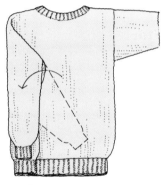

3 Now double the sleeve back to form a straight side edge.

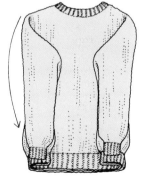

4 Repeat steps 2 and 3 for the opposite side.

5 Fold the garment in half and store.

Index

ACKNOWLEDGEMENTS

Acknowledgements

I should like to thank everyone who has contributed their talents in the making of this book. In particular, my editor Janice Lacock for her enthusiasm, knowledge, organisation and brilliant efficiency. The illustrators Kate Simunek, Mary Tomlin and Coral Mula for cleverly and patiently interpreting my references and requests. Sue Roberts for knitting the samples without fuss and in no time at all, as usual. To my mother for teaching me to knit when I was a child and so starting me off on the path to creative pleasure. And finally to my own family, especially my husband, Dick, who has supported and encouraged me thoroughout my career.

The publishers would also like to thank the following for their help: Creativity (45 New Oxford Street, London WC1) for supplying yarn; Paul Forrester for photography; Peter Barber for the index; Linda Sonntag for proofreading; and Camilla Hughes and Artyfacts for design services.

Photographic acknowledgements
The publishers wish to thank the following for supplying photographs for this book:
Page 9 Pat Morris; 10 ZEFA; 11 Michael Holford; 12 ZEFA; 37 Ann Ronan Picture Library; 39 Courtesy Sirdar (right), Courtesy Patons & Baldwins (left); 112 Illustrated London News Picture Library; 116 Courtesy Sirdar; 138 Hulton-Deutsch Collection; 158 Bridgeman Art Library.
Cover Courtesy Sirdar

All other photographs by Paul Forrester

Picture research: Elaine Willis

Illustrators
Jeremy Gower 140, 184–5
Coral Mula 119–31, 145–6, 148–9
Kate Simunek 40–89, 98–100, 142–4, 154–5, 170–83
Mary Tomlin 18–36, 90–7, 101–14, 147, 150–2, 159–68, 186–9